Leaders and Innovators

Wiley & SAS Business Series

The Wiley & SAS Business Series presents books that help senior-level managers with their critical management decisions.

Titles in the Wiley & SAS Business Series include:

Agile by Design: An Implementation Guide to Analytic Lifecycle Management by Rachel Alt-Simmons

Analytics in a Big Data World: The Essential Guide to Data Science and its Applications by Bart Baesens

Bank Fraud: Using Technology to Combat Losses by Revathi Subramanian

Big Data, Big Innovation: Enabling Competitive Differentiation through Business Analytics by Evan Stubbs

Business Forecasting: Practical Problems and Solutions edited by Michael Gilliland, Len Tashman, and Udo Sglavo

Business Intelligence Applied: Implementing an Effective Information and Communications Technology Infrastructure by Michael Gendron

Business Intelligence and the Cloud: Strategic Implementation Guide by Michael S. Gendron

Business Transformation: A Roadmap for Maximizing Organizational Insights by Aiman Zeid

Data-Driven Healthcare: How Analytics and BI Are Transforming the Industry by Laura Madsen

Delivering Business Analytics: Practical Guidelines for Best Practice by Evan Stubbs

Demand-Driven Forecasting: A Structured Approach to Forecasting, Second Edition by Charles Chase

Demand-Driven Inventory Optimization and Replenishment: Creating a More Efficient Supply Chain by Robert A. Davis

Developing Human Capital: Using Analytics to Plan and Optimize Your Learning and Development Investments by Gene Pease, Barbara Beresford, and Lew Walker

Economic and Business Forecasting: Analyzing and Interpreting Econometric Results by John Silvia, Azhar Iqbal, Kaylyn Swankoski, Sarah Watt, and Sam Bullard

Financial Institution Advantage and the Optimization of Information Processing by Sean C. Keenan

Financial Risk Management: Applications in Market, Credit, Asset, and Liability Management and Firmwide Risk by Jimmy Skoglund and Wei Chen

Fraud Analytics Using Descriptive, Predictive, and Social Network Techniques: A Guide to Data Science for Fraud Detection by Bart Baesens, Veronique Van Vlasselaer, and Wouter Verbeke

Harness Oil and Gas Big Data with Analytics: Optimize Exploration and Production with Data Driven Models by Keith Holdaway

Health Analytics: Gaining the Insights to Transform Health Care by Jason Burke

Heuristics in Analytics: A Practical Perspective of What Influences Our Analytical World by Carlos Andre, Reis Pinheiro, and Fiona McNeill

Hotel Pricing in a Social World: Driving Value in the Digital Economy by Kelly McGuire

Implement, Improve and Expand Your Statewide Longitudinal Data System: Creating a Culture of Data in Education by Jamie McQuiggan and Armistead Sapp

Killer Analytics: Top 20 Metrics Missing from Your Balance Sheet by Mark Brown

Mobile Learning: A Handbook for Developers, Educators, and Learners by Scott McQuiggan, Lucy Kosturko, Jamie McQuiggan, and Jennifer Sabourin

*The Patient Revolution: How Big Data and Analytics Are Transforming the Healthcare Exp*erience by Krisa Tailor

Predictive Analytics for Human Resources by Jac Fitz-enz and John Mattox II

Predictive Business Analytics: Forward-Looking Capabilities to Improve Business Performance by Lawrence Maisel and Gary Cokins

Statistical Thinking: Improving Business Performance, Second Edition, by Roger W. Hoerl and Ronald D. Snee

Too Big to Ignore: The Business Case for Big Data by Phil Simon

Trade-Based Money Laundering: The Next Frontier in International Money Laundering Enforcement by John Cassara

The Visual Organization: Data Visualization, Big Data, and the Quest for Better Decisions by Phil Simon

Understanding the Predictive Analytics Lifecycle by Al Cordoba

Unleashing Your Inner Leader: An Executive Coach Tells All by Vickie Bevenour

Using Big Data Analytics: Turning Big Data into Big Money by Jared Dean

Visual Six Sigma, Second Edition, by Ian Cox, Marie Gaudard, Philip Ramsey, Mia Stephens, and Leo Wright

For more information on any of the above titles, please visit www.wiley.com.

Leaders and Innovators

How Data-Driven Organizations Are Winning with Analytics

Tho H. Nguyen

WILEY

Published by John Wiley & Sons, Inc., Hoboken, New Jersey.

Published simultaneously in Canada.

Library of Congress Cataloging-in-Publication Data is available:

ISBN 9781119232575 (Hardcover)
ISBN 9781119276913 (ePDF)
ISBN 9781119276920 (ePub)

Cover design: Wiley

Cover image: ©aleksandarvelasevic/iStock.com

Printed in the United States of America

10 9 8 7 6 5 4 3 2 1

This book is dedicated to Ánh, Ana, and family, who provided their unconditional love and support with all the crazy, late nights and frantic weekends it took to complete this book.

Contents

Foreword

By James Taylor

I have been working with advanced analytics since 2001 and have watched the market evolve and mature over the intervening years. Where once only banks focused on predictive analytics to manage risk, now companies across all industries do. The role of advanced analytics in managing the customer journey has gone from innovative to mainstream. The time to develop and deploy advanced analytics has gone from months to seconds, even as the amount of data being analyzed has exploded. Leading companies see analytics as a core competency, not just a point solution, and innovators are increasingly looking at data as a source of future innovation. How to become data-driven and win with analytics is on everyone's to-do list, and books like the one Tho has written are critical in developing a practical plan to achieve data-driven, analytic innovation.

Tho and I met a few years ago when we co-presented on analytics through our work as faculty members of the International Institute for Analytics. We have a shared interest in the technologies and approaches that are both driving the increased use of analytics in organizations and responding to the increased demand from organizations of every size and in every industry.

All organizations have data, and we live in an era where organizations have more of this data digitized and accessible than ever before. More digital channels and more devices generate digital exhaust about our customers, partners, suppliers, and even our equipment. Government and third-party data are increasingly accessible, with marketplaces and APIs making yet more data available to us. Our ability to store and analyze text, audio, image, and video data expands our reach yet further. All these data stretch our data infrastructure to the limit and beyond, driving the adoption of new technologies like in-database and in-memory analytics and Hadoop. But simply storing and managing the data is not enough. To succeed, we need to use the data to drive better decision making. This means we need to understand it, analyze it, and deploy the resulting insights so that they can be acted on. These new technologies must be integrated into an end-to-end data and analytic life cycle if they are to add value.

Over the years, I have spoken with literally hundreds of organizations that are using analytics to improve their decision making. I have helped train thousands of people in the key techniques and skills required for successful adoption of analytic technology. My experience is that organizations that can think coherently about their decision making, especially their day-to-day operational decision making, and can see huge benefits from making those decisions more analytically— from using their data to see what will work and what will not. Such a data-driven approach to decision making drives a degree of innovation in organizations second to none. Succeeding and innovating with analytical decision-making, however, requires a coherent approach to the analytic life cycle and the effective adoption of data management and analytic technologies.

With this book, Tho has provided an overview of the analytical life cycle and technologies required to deliver data-driven analytic innovation. He begins with an overview of the analytical data life cycle, the journey from data exploration to data preparation, analytic model development and ultimately deployment into an organization's decision making, involved to transform data into strategic insights using analytics. This sets the scene for chapters on the critical technology categories that are transforming how organizations manage and use data. Each of these technologies is considered and put in its correct place in the life cycle supported by real customer examples of the value to be gained.

First, in-database processing integrates advanced analytics into a database or data warehouse so data can be analyzed in situ. Eliminating the time and cost of moving data from where it is stored to somewhere it can be analyzed both reduces elapsed time and allows for more data to be processed in business-realistic time frames. Improved accuracy and reduced time to value are the result.

In-memory analytics delivers incredibly fast response to complex analytical problems to reduce time to analyze data. Increasing speed in this way allows for more iterations, more approaches to understanding the data, and greater likelihood of finding useful insight. This increased speed can also be used to analyze fast-changing or streaming data without waiting for the data to be stored somewhere.

Finally, the Hadoop big data ecosystem allows for the collection and management of more data (both structured and semi-structured) than ever before. Organizations that might once have thrown away or archived data perceived as low value can now store and access data cost-effectively. Integrated with traditional data storage techniques, Hadoop allows for broader and more flexible data management across the organization.

These new approaches are combined with an overview of some more traditional techniques to bring it all together at the end with a description of the kind of collaborative data architecture and effective analytic data life cycle required. A final chapter discusses the impact of cloud computing, cyber-security, the Internet of Things (IoT), cognitive computing, and the move to "everything as a service" business models on data and analytics.

If you are one of those business and IT professionals trying to learn how to use data to drive innovation in your organizations and become leaders in your industry, then you need an overview of the data management and analytical processes critical to data-driven success. This book will give you that overview, introduce you to critical best practices, and show you how real companies have already used these processes to succeed.

James Taylor is CEO and principal consultant, Decision Management Solutions, and a faculty member of the International Institute for Analytics. He is the author of Decision Management Systems: A Practical Guide to Using Business Rules and Predictive Analytics *(IBM Press, 2012). He also wrote* Smart (Enough) Systems *(Prentice Hall, 2007) with Neil Raden and* The Microguide to Process and Decision Modeling in BPMN/DMN *with Tom Debevoise. James is an active consultant, educator, speaker, and writer working with companies all over the world. He is based in Palo Alto, California, and can be reached at james@decisionmanagementsolutions.com.*

Acknowledgments

First, I would like to recognize you, the reader of this book. Thank you for your interest to learn and to become leaders and innovators within your organization. I am contributing the proceeds to worthy causes that focus on technology and science to improve the world, from fighting hunger to advocating education to innovating social change.

There are many people who deserve heartfelt credit for assisting me in writing this book. This book would have not happened without the ultimate support and guidance from my esteemed colleagues and devoted customers from around the world. A sincere appreciation to my friends at Teradata and SAS, who encouraged me to write this book and helped me to validate with the technical details and to keep it simple for nontechnical readers to understand.

I owe a huge amount of gratitude to the people who reviewed and provided input word by word, chapter by chapter—specifically, Shelley Sessoms, Bob Matsey, and Paul Segal. Reading pages of technical jargons, trying to follow my thoughts, and translating my words in draft form can be a daunting challenge, but you did it with grace, patience, and swiftness. Thank you for the fantastic input that helped me to fine-tune the message.

A sincere appreciation goes to all marketing professionals, IT professionals, and business professionals who I have interacted with over the years. You have welcomed me, helped me to learn, allowed me to contribute, and provided insights in this book. Finally, to all my family (the Nguyen and Dang crew), the St. Francis Episcopalian sponsors, the Rotary Club (the Jones Family, the Veale Family)—they all have contributed to my success, and I would not be where I am today without them. To my wife and daughter, thank you for being the love of my life and the light of my day.

Tho H. Nguyen

About the Author

Tho Nguyen came to the United States in 1980 as a refugee from Vietnam with his parents, six sisters, and one brother. Sponsored by the St. Francis Episcopal Church in Greensboro, North Carolina, Tho had abundant guidance and support from his American family who taught him English and acclimated him to an exciting and promising life in America.

Tho holds a Bachelor of Science in Computer Engineering from North Carolina State University and an MBA degree in International Business from the University of Bristol, England. During his MBA studies, Tho attended L'École Nationale des Ponts et Chaussées (ENPC) in Paris, University of Hong Kong, and Berkeley University in California. Tho proudly represented the Rotary Club as an Ambassadorial Scholar which provided him a fresh perspective and a deep appreciation of the world.

With more than 18 years in the Information Technology industry, Tho works closely with technology partners, research and development, and customers globally to drive and deliver value-added business solutions in analytics, data warehousing, and data management. Integrating his technical and business background, Tho has extensive experience in product management, global marketing, and business alliance and strategy management. Tho is a faculty member of the International Institute for Analytics, an active presenter at various conferences, and a blogger on data management and analytics.

In his spare time, Tho enjoys spending time with his family, traveling, running, and playing tennis. He is an avid foodie who is very adventurous and likes to taste cuisines around the world.

Introduction

Data management and analytic practices have changed dramatically since I entered the industry in 1998. Data volumes are exploding beyond imagination, easily in the petabytes. There are many varieties of data that we are collecting, both structured and semi-structured data. We are acquiring data at much higher velocity, demanding daily renewal, sometimes even hourly. As the Greek philosopher Heraclitus so wisely stated centuries ago, "The only thing that is constant is change."

WHY YOU SHOULD READ THIS BOOK

The management of data, and how we handle and analyze it, has changed dramatically since the start of the "big data" era. Ultimately, all of the data must deliver information for decision making. It is definitely an exciting time that creates many challenges but also great opportunities for all of us to explore and adopt new and disruptive technologies to help with data management and analytical needs. And, now, the journey of this book begins.

I have attended a number of conferences where I have been able to share with both business and IT audiences the technologies that can help them more effectively manage their data, in return creating a more streamlined analytical life cycle. I have learned from customers the challenges they encounter and the fascinating things they are doing with agile analytics to drive innovation and gain competitive advantage for their companies. These are the biggest and most common themes:

- "How can I integrate data management and analytical process into a unified environment to make my processes run faster?"
- "I do NOT have days or weeks to prepare my data for analysis."
- "My analytical process takes days and weeks to complete, and by the time it is completed, the information is outdated."

- "My staff is spending too much time with tactical data management tasks and not enough time focusing on strategic analytical exploration."
- "What I can do to retain my staff from leaving because their work is no longer challenging?"
- "My data is scattered all over. Where do I go to get the most current version of the data for analysis?"

A good friend of mine, who is an editor, approached me to consider writing a book that combines real-world customer successes based on the concepts they adopted from presentations and white papers that I authored over the years. After a few months of developing the abstracts, outlines, and chapters, we agreed to proceed publishing this book with a focus on customer success stories in each section. My goals for this book are to:

- Educate on what innovative technologies are available for integrating data management and analytics in a cohesive environment.
- Inform about what fascinating technologies leading edge companies are adopting and implementing to help them solve some of the big data challenges.
- Share customer case studies and successes across industries such as retail, banking, telecommunications, e-commerce, and transportation.

Whether you are from business or IT, I believe you will appreciate the real-world best practices and use cases that you can leverage in your profession. These best practices have been proven to help provide faster data-driven insights and decisions.

Writing this book was a privilege and honor. Mixed feelings went through my head as I started writing the book even though I was excited about sharing my experiences and customer successes with other IT and business professionals. The reasons for the mixed feelings were twofold:

1. Will the technology discussed in this book still be considered as innovative or relevant when the book is published?
2. How can I bring value to the readers who consider themselves to be innovators and leaders in the IT market?

Customer interactions are very important to me and a highlight in my profession. I have talked to many customers globally, tried to understand their business problems, and advised them on the appropriate technologies and solutions to solve their issues. I also have traveled around the world, sharing with customers and prospects the latest technologies and innovation in the market and how some of the leading-edge companies have adopted them to be more competitive and become the pioneers of managing data and applying analytics in a unified environment. Before I dive into the details, I believe it is appropriate to set the tone and definitions to be referenced throughout this book and some trends in the industry that demand inventive technologies to sustain leadership in a competitive, global economy. The topics of this book are focused on data management and analytics and how to unite these two elements into one single entity for optimal performance, economics, and governance—all of which are key initiatives for business and IT in many corporations.

LET'S START WITH DEFINITIONS

The term *data management* has been around for a long time and has transformed into many other trendy buzzwords over the years. However, for simplification purposes, I will use the term *data management* since it is the foundation for this book. I define data management as a process by which data are acquired, integrated, and stored for data users to access. Data management is often associated with the ETL (extraction, transformation, and load) process to prepare the data for the database or warehouse. The ETL process is very much embedded into the data management environment. The ultimate result from the ETL process is to satisfy data users with reliable and timely data for analytics.

There are many definitions for analytics, and the focus on analytics has recently been on the rise. Its popularity has reemerged since the 1990s because many companies across industries have recognized the value of analytics and the field of data analysis to analyze the past, present, and future with data. *Analytics* can be very broad and has become the catch-all term for a variety of different business initiatives. According to Gartner, analytics is used to describe statistical and mathematical data analysis that clusters, segments, scores, and predicts what scenarios have happened, are happening, or are most likely to happen.[1] Analytics have become the link between IT and business to exploit massive mounds of data. Based on my interactions with customers, I define analytics as a process of analyzing large amounts of data to gain knowledge and understanding about your business and deliver data-driven decisions to make business improvements or changes within an organization.

INDUSTRY TRENDS AND CHALLENGES

Now that the definitions have been established, let's examine the state of the IT industry and what customers are sharing with me regarding the challenges they encounter in their organizations:

- *Data as a differentiator and an asset*: Forbes Research concurs that data is a differentiator and an asset.[2] As an industry, we are data rich but knowledge poor because organizations are unable to make sense of all the data they collect. We are barely scratching the surface when it comes to analyzing all of the data that we have access to or can acquire. In addition, the ability to analyze the data has become much more complex, and companies may not have the right infrastructure and/or tools to do the job effectively and efficiently. As data volumes continue to grow, it is imperative to have the proper foundation for managing big data and beyond.
- *Analytics for everything*: Customers demand real-time analytics to empower data-driven decisions from CEO to a factory operator. Based on recent TechRepublic research, 70 percent of the respondents use analytics in some shape or form to drive performance and decisions. Whether it is to open a brand new division or develop another product line, the right decision will have a significant impact on the bottom line and, ultimately, the organization's success. As business becomes more targeted, personalized, and public, it is vital to make precise, fact-based (data-driven), transparent decisions. These decisions need to have an auditable history to show regulatory compliance and risk management.

- *The "now" factor*: It seems that the X factor that a company should possess is to have immediate availability of products and services for their consumers. For example, the retail industry is facing the "now" factor challenge. Extremely low prices and great services are no longer enough to attract consumers. Businesses need to have what consumers are looking for such as color, size, and fit—when they need it. That is the key to attract and retain customers for success. Consumers are willing to pay at a premium on product availability. Based on a retail survey from *Forbes*, 58 percent said availability is more important than price, and 92 percent said they will not wait for products to come into stock. Companies must outsmart their competition and be able to share information with customers for products and services readiness.

These trends translate into challenges and opportunities for companies in every industry. The customers that I deal with consider these as their top three challenges:

- *Database performance*: With a database architecture that may not scale to match the amount of data, it's difficult to process full data sets—or accomplish data discovery, analysis, and visualization activities.
- *Analytical capabilities*: Because of inept data access and time consuming data preparation, analysts tend to focus on solving access issues instead of running tactical analytical processes and strategic tasks. In addition, there is an inability to develop and process complex analytic models fast enough to keep up with economic changes.
- *Data quality and integration*: Having a multitude of data variety, silo data marts, and localized data extracts makes it difficult to get a handle on exactly how much data there is and what kind. When data are not in one location and/or data management is disjointed, its quality is questionable. When quality is questionable, results are uncertain.

Data is every organization's strategic asset. Data provide information for operational and strategic decisions. Because we are collecting many more types of data (from websites, social media, mobile, sensors, etc.) and the speed at which we collect the data has significantly accelerated, data volumes have grown exponentially. Customers that I have spoken to have doubled their data volumes in less than 24 months, which is beyond what Moore's law (that the rate of change doubles in 24 months) predicted over 50 years ago. With the pace of change escalating faster than ever, customers are looking for the latest innovation in technologies to try and satisfy their needs in both IT and business within a corporation and transform every challenge into big opportunities to positively impact the profitability and bottom line. I truly believe the new and innovative technologies such as in-database processing, in-memory analytics, and the emerging Hadoop technology will help tame the challenges of managing big data, uncover new opportunities with analytics, and deliver a higher return on investment by augmenting data management with integrated analytics.

WHO SHOULD READ THIS BOOK?

This book is for business and IT professionals who want to learn about new and innovative technologies and learn what their peers have done to be successful in their line of work. It is for the business analysts who want to be smarter at delivering information to different parts of the organization. It is for the data scientists who want to explore new ways to apply analytics. It is for managers, directors, and executives who want to innovate and leverage analytics to make data-driven decisions impacting profitability and the livelihood of their business.

You should read this book if your profession is in one of these groups:

- Executive managers, including chief executive officers, chief operating officers, chief strategy officers, chief marketing officers, or any other company leader, who want to innovate and drive efficiency or deliver strategic goals
- Line of business managers that oversee existing technologies and want to adopt new technologies for the company
- Sales managers and account directors who want to introduce new concepts and technologies to their customers

- Business professions such as business analysts, program managers, and offer managers who analyze data and deliver information to the leadership team for decision making
- IT professionals who manage the data, ensuring data quality and integration, so that the data can be available for analytics

This book is ideal for professions who want to improve the data management and analytical processes of their organization, explore new capabilities by applying analytics directly to the data, and learn from others how to be innovative and to become pioneers in their organization.

HOW TO READ THIS BOOK

This book can be read in a linear manner, chapter by chapter. It proceeds very much as a process of crawling, walking, sprinting, then running. However, if you are a reader who is already familiar with the concept of in-database processing, in-memory analytics, or Hadoop, you can simply skip to the chapter that is most relevant to your situation. If you are not familiar with any of the topics, I highly suggest starting with Chapter 1, as it highlights the analytical life cycle of the data and data's typical journey to become information and insights for your organization. You can proceed to Chapters 2 to 4 (*crawl, walk, sprint*) to see how specific technologies can be applied directly to the data. Chapter 5 (how to *run* the relay) brings all of the elements together and how each technology can help to manage big data and advanced analytics. Chapter 6 discusses the top five focus areas in data management and analytics as well as possible future technologies.

Table 1 provides a description and focus for each chapter.

LET YOUR JOURNEY BEGIN

An organization's most valuable asset is its customers. Yet right next to customers are those precious assets that the enterprise can leverage to attract, retain, and interact with those valuable customers for profitable growth: your *data*. Every organization that I have encountered has huge, tidal waves of data—streaming in like waves from every

Table 1 Outline of the Chapters

Chapter	Description	Takeaway
1. The Analytical Data Life Cycle	The purpose of this chapter is to illustrate the typical life cycle of data and the stages (data exploration, data preparation, model development, and model deployment) involved to transform data into strategic insights using analytics.	■ What is the analytical data life cycle? ■ What are the characteristics of each stage of the life cycle? ■ What technologies are best suited for each stage of the data?
2. In-Database Processing	This purpose of this chapter is to provide the reader with the concept of in-database processing. In-database processing refers to the integration of advanced analytics into the database or data warehousing. With this capability, analytic processing is optimized to run where the data reside, in parallel, without having to copy or move the data for analysis.	■ What is in-database processing? ■ Why in-database processing? ■ What process should leverage in-database? ■ What are some best practices? ■ What are some use cases and success stories? ■ What are the benefits of using in-database analytics?
3. In-Memory Analytics	This purpose of this chapter is to provide the reader the concept of in-memory analytics. This latest innovation provides an entirely new approach to tackle big data by using an in-memory analytics engine to deliver super-fast responses to complex analytical problems.	■ What is in-memory analytics? ■ Why in-memory analytics? ■ What process should leverage in-memory analytics? ■ What are some best practices? ■ What are some use cases and success stories? ■ What are the benefits of using in-memory analytics?
4. Hadoop and Big Data	This purpose of this chapter is to explain the value of Hadoop. Organizations are faced with the unique big data challenges collecting more data than ever before, both structured and semi-structured data. There has never been a greater need for proactive and agile strategies to manage and integrate big data.	■ What is Hadoop? ■ Why Hadoop in big data environment? ■ How does Hadoop play in the modern architecture? ■ What are some best practices? ■ What are some use cases and success stories? ■ What are the benefits of using Hadoop in big data?

Table 1 *(Continued)*

Chapter	Description	Takeaway
5. End-to-End – Bringing it All Together	This purpose of this chapter is to summarize and bring together the various technologies and concepts shared in Chapters 2–4. Combining traditional methods with modern and new approaches can save time and money for any organization.	■ How are in-database analytics, in-memory analytics, and Hadoop complementary? ■ What are use cases and customer success stories? ■ What are some benefits of an integrated data management and analytic architecture?
6. Conclusion and Forward Thoughts	This purpose of this chapter is to conclude the book with the power of having an end-to-end data management and analytics platform for delivering data-driven decisions. It also provides final thoughts about the future of technologies.	■ What is the future for data management? ■ What is the future for analytics? ■ What are the top five focus areas in data management and analytics?

direction—from multiple channels and a variety of sources. Data are everywhere—as far as the eye can see! All day, every day, data flow into and through the business and your database or data warehouse environment. Now, let's examine how all your data can be analyzed in an efficient and effective process to deliver data-driven decisions.

ENDNOTES

1. Gartner, "Analytics," *IT Glossary*, http://www.gartner.com/it-glossary/analytics/.
2. Forbes Insight, *Betting on Big Data* (Jersey City, NJ: Forbes Insights, 2015), http://images.forbes.com/forbesinsights/StudyPDFs/Teradata-BettingOnBigData-REPORT.pdf.

CHAPTER 1

The Analytical Data Life Cycle

Like all things, there is a beginning and an ending in every journey. The same can be said about your data. Thus, all data have a life cycle—from inception to end of life and the analytical data life cycle is no different. In my interactions with customers, they tend to relate to four stages (data exploration, data preparation, model development, and model deployment) as the framework for managing the analytical data life cycle. Each stage is critical, as it supports the entire life cycle linearly. For example, model development cannot happen effectively if you do not prepare and explore the data beforehand. Figure 1.1 illustrates the analytical data life cycle.

Each phase of the lifecycle requires a specific role within the organization. For example, the IT's role is to get all data in one place. Business analysts step in during the data exploration and data preparation processes. Data scientists, data modelers, and statisticians are often involved in the model development stage. Finally, business analysts and/or IT can be a part of the model deployment process. Let's examine each stage of the analytical data life cycle.

STAGE 1: DATA EXPLORATION

The first and very critical stage is data exploration. Data exploration is the process that summarizes the characteristics of the data and extracts knowledge from the data. This process is typically conducted by a business analyst who wants to explore:

- What the data look like
- What variables are in the data set
- Whether there are any missing observations

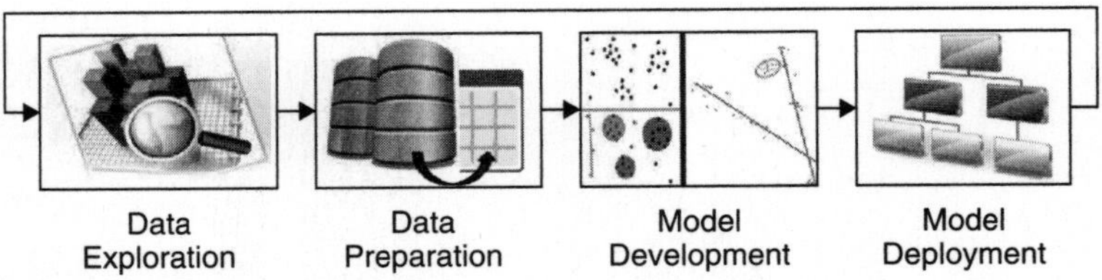

Figure 1.1 Analytical data life cycle

- How the data are related
- What are some of the data patterns
- Does the data fit with other data being explored?
- Do you have all of the data that you need for analysis?

An initial exploration of the data helps to explain these common inquiries. It also permits analysts to become more familiar and intimate with the data that they want to analyze.

The data exploration process normally involves a data visualization tool. In recent years, data visualization tools have become very popular among business analysts for data exploration purposes because they provide an eye-catching user interface that allows users to quickly and easily view most of the important features of the data. From this step, users can identify variables that are likely good candidates to explore and provide value to the other data that you are interested in for analysis. Data visualization tools offer many attractive features, and one of them is the ability to display the data graphically—for example, scatter plots or bar charts/pie charts. With the graphical displays of the data, users can determine if two or more variables correlate and whether they are relevant for further in-depth analysis.

The data exploration stage is critical. Customers who have opted to skip this stage tend to experience many issues in the later phases of the analytical life cycle. One of the best practices is to explore all your data directly in the database that allows the users to know the data before extracting for analysis, eliminate redundancy, and remove irrelevant data for analytics. The ability to quickly extract knowledge from large complex data sets provides an advantage for the data preparation stage.

STAGE 2: DATA PREPARATION

The second stage of the analytical life cycle is data preparation. Data preparation is the process of collecting, integrating, and aggregating the data into one file or data table for use in analytics. This process can be very tedious and cumbersome due some of the following challenges:

- Combining data from numerous sources
- Handling inconsistent or nonstandardized data
- Cleaning dirty data

- Integrating data that was manually entered
- Dealing with structured and semistructured data
- Value of the data

Customers that I have dealt with spend as much as 85 percent of their time preparing the data in the stage of the life cycle. The data preparation normally involves an IT specialist working closely with a business analyst to thoroughly understand their data needs. They say that preparing data generally involves fixing any errors (typically from human and/or machine input), filling in nulls and/or incomplete data, and merging/joining data from various sources or data formats. These activities consume many resources and personnel hours.

Data preparation is often directed to harmonize, enrich, and standardize your data in the database. In a common scenario, you may have multiple values that are used in a data set to represent the same value. An example of this is seen with U.S. states—where various values may be commonly used to represent the same state. A state like North Carolina could be represented by "NC," "N.C.," "N. Carolina,"' or "North Carolina," to name a few. A data preparation tool could be leveraged in this example to identify an incorrect number of distinctive values (in the case of U.S. states, a unique count greater than 50 would raise a flag, as there are only 50 states in the United States). These values would then need to be standardized to use only an acceptable or standard abbreviation or only full spelling in every row.

Data preparation creates the right data for the model development process. Without the right data, you may be developing an incomplete data model on which to make your decisions. In a worst-case scenario where you have the incorrect data for the analytic data model, you will get erroneous results that send you down the path of a devastating decision. Bringing all the data from different sources and ensuring that the data are cleansed and integrated are the core building blocks to a complete analytical data model for decision support.

STAGE 3: MODEL DEVELOPMENT

Now that you have explored and prepared the data, it is time to develop the analytical data model. Before discussing the model development cycle, it is worthwhile to provide business pains faced by many organizations that develop a large number of analytical data models. Data models can take days, weeks, and even months to complete. The complexity is due to the availability of the data, the time it takes to generate the analytical data model, and the fact that models can be too large to maintain and in a constant state of decay.

To add to the complexity, model development involves many team members—data modelers, data architects, data scientists, business analyst, validation testers, and model scoring officers. Many organizations are challenged with the process of signing off on the development, validation, storage, and retirement of the data model. Model decay is another challenge that organizations encounter, so they need to constantly know how old the model is, who developed the model, and who is using the model for what application. The ability to version-control the model over time is another critical business need that includes event logging, tracking changes to the data attributes, and understanding how the model form and usage evolve over time. It also addresses what to do with the retired models—possibly archiving them for auditability, traceability, and regulatory compliance.

The use of an analytical data model varies from customer to customer. It is dependent on the industry or vertical that you are in; for example, you might have to adhere to regulations such as Sarbanes-Oxley or Basel II. Customers commonly leverage their analytical data models to examine

- Customer retention
- Customer attrition/churn
- Marketing response
- Consumer loyalty and offers
- Fraud detection
- Credit scoring
- Risk management
- Lifetime value
- Path to purchase
- Drug development
- Clinical trials
- Anti-money laundering

- Demand forecasting
- Loss prevention

If you are in the banking/financial industry, you may develop a data model that looks at time since last payment, number of missed payments, ratio of accrued interest, or formal loan cancellation to analyze risk of a loan default application. For retail and telecommunications, you may want to develop a data model that looks at customer acquisition/churn and cross-sell opportunities that rely on response to previous promotions within some time period and/or through some channels to enhance customer experience. Regardless of the data model type or industry, the data used in the analytical data model must be up to date and available during the lifetime of the model development and scoring processes.

Analytical data models have the ability to uncover hidden opportunities and are considered to be the fundamental success of a business. The use of analytics is increasing at an exponential rate, and organizations are developing analytical data models to enable data-driven decisions. Once models are built, deploying the models provides the outputs (results) that are driving many operational processes throughout the organizations.

STAGE 4: MODEL DEPLOYMENT

Once the model is built, it is time to deploy the model. Deploying a model often implicates scoring of the analytical data model. The process of executing a model to make predictions about behavior that has yet to happen is called *scoring*. Thus, the output of the model that is often the prediction is called a *score*. Scores can be in any form—from numbers to strings to entire data structures. The most common scores are numbers such as

- Probability of responding to a particular promotional offer
- Risk of an applicant defaulting on a loan
- Propensity to pay off a debt
- Likelihood a customer leave/churn
- Probability to buy a product

Scoring as part of the model deployment stage is the unglamorous pillar of analytical data life cycle. It is not as thrilling or exciting as the model development stage, where you may incorporate a neural network or a regression algorithm. Without the scoring and model deployment, the analytical data model is shelfware and is pretty useless. At the end of the day, however, scoring your analytical data model will reveal the information to enable you to make data-driven decisions.

The application that is used to execute the scoring process is typically simpler than the ones used to develop the models. This is because the statistical and analytical functions and optimization procedures that were used to build the model are no longer needed; all that is required is a piece of software that can evaluate mathematical functions on a set of data inputs from the analytical data model.

The scoring process invokes a software application (often called the *scoring engine*), which then takes an analytical data model and a data set to produce a set of scores for the records in the data set. There are three common approaches to scoring an analytical data model:

1. A scoring engine software application that is separate from the model-development application
2. A scoring engine that is part of the model-development application
3. A scoring engine that is produced by executing the data model code (e.g., SAS, C++, or Java) that is output by the model development application

The type of model generated will depend on the model development software that is used. Some software can produce multiple types of models, whereas others will generate only a single type. In the first two approaches, the scoring engine is a software application that needs to be run by the user. It might have a graphical user interface or it might be a command line program, in which the user specifies the input parameters by typing them onto a console interface when the program is run. There are usually three inputs to the scoring engine: the model that is to be run, the data to be scored, and the location where the output scores should be put.

In the third approach of the scoring engine, the model acts as its own scoring engine. After the model development software generates the model, it will need to be compiled into an executable form. This step is usually done manually and often requires technical knowledge of system and programming level details. The main reason to use a compiled model is to increase performance because a compiled data model will usually run significantly faster than a model that requires a separate scoring engine.

The analysts often use a model development software application that generates model-scoring code in a particular programming language. Perhaps due to company policy or data compliance, the IT department scoring officer might convert the scoring code to another language. Code conversion introduces the potential for loss in translation, which results in costly errors. A single error in the model-scoring logic results or the data attribute selection can easily deliver an incorrect output, which can cost the company millions of dollars. Converting the scoring algorithm is usually a slow manual process producing thousands of lines of code. It is best to avoid this scenario, and customers should consider selecting the model development and deployment software application that is harmonious and compatible.

END-TO-END PROCESS

I have defined the stages and characteristics of the analytical data life cycle. Figure 1.2 shows what technologies are best suited for each stage.

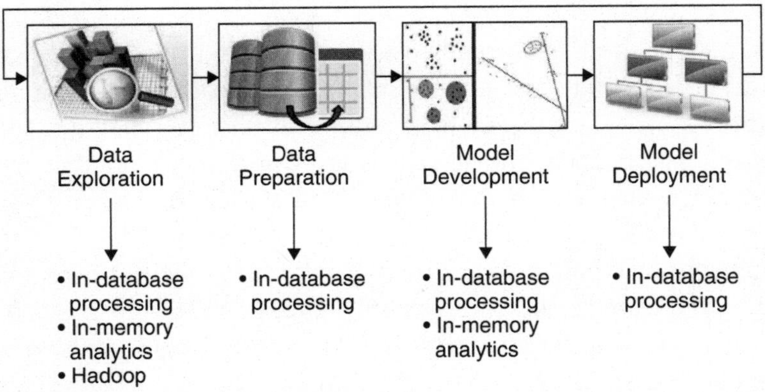

Figure 1.2 Technologies for the analytical data life cycle

In the next few chapters, I will go into details of how and why you should consider using these technologies in each of the stages. In addition, I will share anecdotes from customers who discover value in performance, economics, and governance with each technology at different stages. Each technology enables you to analyze your data faster and allows you to crawl, walk, sprint, and run through the journey of the analytical data life cycle. Your journey starts now.

CHAPTER 2

In-Database Processing

It is a known fact that organizations are collecting more structured and semi-structured data than ever before, and it is presenting great opportunities and challenges to analyze ALL of this complex data. In this volatile and competitive economy, there has never been a bigger need for proactive and agile strategies to overcome these challenges by applying the analytics directly to the data rather than shuffling data around. The point: There are two key technologies that dramatically improve and increase performance when analyzing big data: *in-database* and *in-memory* analytics. I will focus on the in-database analytics (processing) in this chapter.

BACKGROUND

The concept of in-database processing was introduced in the mid-1990s, and vendors such as Teradata, IBM, and Oracle made it commercially available as object-related database systems. The in-database capabilities were still in its infancy and did not really catch on with customers until the mid-2000s. The concept of migrating analytics from the analytical workstation or personal computers and into a centralized enterprise data warehouse sounded good and promising, but customers were very wary of how it could work within their processes and cultures. In addition, IT and business users were questioning what capabilities were present to add value to their organization, which wanted to adopt the technology. Also occurring at the same time, big data has entered into the industry and become the buzzword and trend in the IT industry. Needless to say, it is the perfect storm for in-database processing to be a great choice to solve business issues.

The need for this technology has become more in-demand as the amount of data available to collect and analyze continues to grow at an alarming rate, largely due to the expansion and use of the Internet and mobile devices. Customers have been collecting data from megabytes to gigabytes or from terabytes to petabytes and beyond. With the speed of data being collected, the need for change from businesses has accelerated where performance gains of hours to seconds can make a difference in the decision making in some industries. In addition, as more people and industries rely on data and analytics to answer important business questions, the questions they ask have become more complex, which mandate more sophisticated technologies and even more precise results. Thus, the insurgence of big data is one of the primary reasons for the growth of in-database processing—an enabling technology to gather, process, and analyze data efficiently and effectively. Let's examine how analytics are being handled currently.

TRADITIONAL APPROACH

Traditionally, in order to analyze data, the data must be extracted from a database or data warehouse to a server or personal computer. Currently, many customers are approaching analytics by moving the data out of databases into a separate analytics environment for processing and then back to the database. Users have been shielded from the fact that traditional approaches to data analysis required the movement of data out of the database for analytical processing. The users have not had to contend with the fact that the conventional approach to analytics has imposed performance constraints as data was moved out of the database and into a separate analytics environment. The result from this process produces duplicate data and redundant data in many places. They may not know where to look since the data is scattered and not centralized. Nor have they had to consider the security issues inherent in moving data from one environment to another. Figure 2.1 illustrates the traditional approach to analytics.

Figure 2.1 shows the common and traditional process and architecture used by many businesses to develop and deploy analytic data model in their infrastructure. In this approach, data are extracted from a variety of sources (mainframes, CRM applications, call centers, etc.) ranging from enterprise data warehouses to data marts across multiple lines of business. The data are collected, transformed, and integrated into a development analytic data set (ADS). The ADS is typically a large flat data structure, such as a flat file, that contains hundreds of candidate variables where each row represents an observation on the unit of interest such as customer (also known as modeling ADS). These data

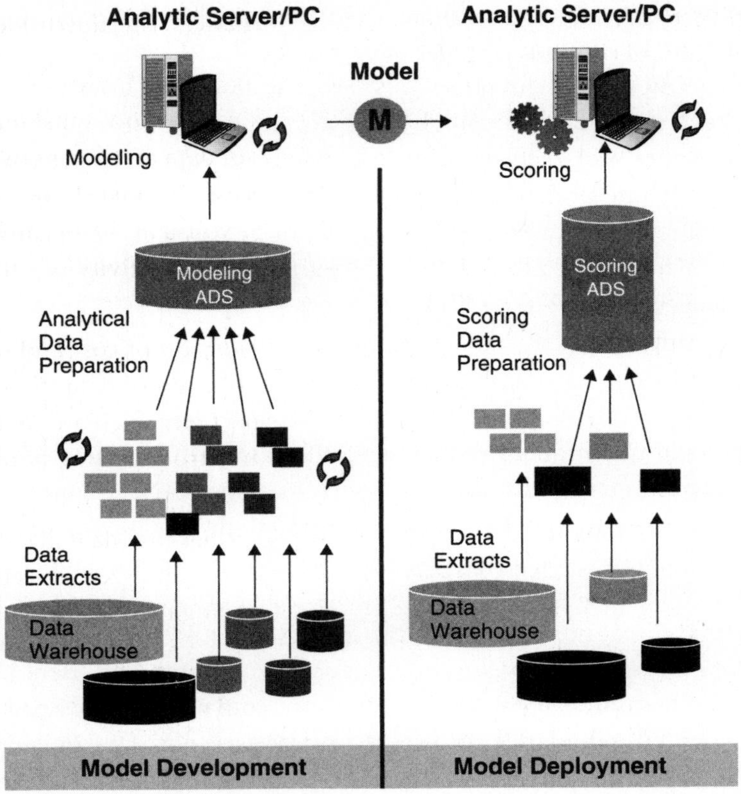

Figure 2.1 Traditional approach to analytics

are then used to develop analytic data models within an analytic environment. Once the model is developed, tested, and validated, it is then exported into the scoring environment that is typically based on production or operational data. For scoring purposes, the data are again extracted and prepared based on model requirements into the "Scoring ADS" (also sometimes referred as the score table). This table only has the variable used in the analytical model variables but may also contain millions of records to be scored. Scoring is often executed on the scoring server.

The traditional approach has many moving parts and processes including lots of data movement and replication. It presents many challenges within an organization—in particular data validation, data quality, performance, economics, and governance. The downside to the traditional process includes:

- Moving the data through the network can be slow—just imagine transferring terabytes or petabytes of data across a network that has limited bandwidth. This process can take hours and days to complete. During this process, you may be negatively impacting your corporate network and productivity of others within the organization.
- Duplicating the data adds another dimension of cost and data silo—by copying millions and billions of rows of data, there is another data set to maintain and support which creates a data silo and adds additional costs to the infrastructure (for storage, backup, etc.).
- Governing the data can be challenging—because data are scattered and collected from many sources to be analyzed, it is cumbersome to govern where the data are being used and how it is being analyzed.

In the traditional process, you have the data management process apart from the analytical application, and they are not likely integrated to provide end-to-end capabilities. As mentioned in the Introduction and Chapter 1, data management is a key element to having effective analysis of the data, and the data preparation process within the data management side can be very time consuming and labor intensive. Having separate processes and disconnected technologies can be costly and not very economical.

Applying the analytics where the data reside and leveraging the power of the database eliminate costs, time, data quality, and security issues associated with the traditional approach by simply processing the analytics in the data warehouse.

IN-DATABASE APPROACH

Most organizations have confessed that there is no shortage of data to analyze. Organizations often have more data than they're even aware of and more data are being collected daily. Of course, the challenge is

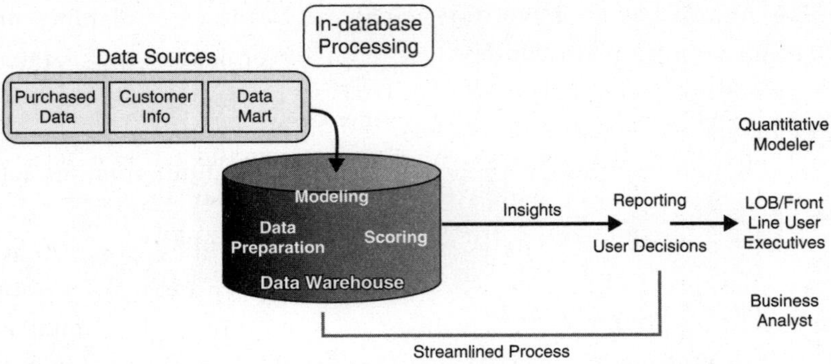

Figure 2.2 In-database approach to analytics

to find the most effective way to process the data, ensure its accuracy, store it in an inexpensive manner, and increase the speed and flexibility with which end users can examine it from multiple perspectives to uncover valuable and strategic insights it contains. The good news is that there is a way: the in-database processing.

In-database processing refers to the integration of advanced analytics into the data warehousing platform functionality. Many analytical computing solutions and large databases use this approach because it provides significant performance improvements over the traditional methods. Thus, many business analysts have adopted in-database processing and have been able to realize the valuable business benefits of streamlined processing and increased performance. Figure 2.2 shows the in-database approach to integrating data management and analytics.

With in-database processing, business analysts and IT users have the ability to explore the data, prepare it for analysis in an analytical data set, develop complex data models, and score the model—the end-to-end data life cycle all within the database or data warehouse. By doing so, it removes the need to either move or extract the data to an environment or convert the analytical code to something that could be executed on the data platform.

THE NEED FOR IN-DATABASE ANALYTICS

An in-database analytics approach is much faster, more efficient, more productive, and more secure than traditional analytics approaches.

In-database analytics delivers immediate performance, scalability, and governance improvements because data never leaves the database until the results are either filtered or processed. One of the main advantages of in-database analytics is eliminating the movement of data. It is accomplished by integrating the analytical functionality with the database.

By leveraging the in-database analytics capabilities, organizations can now make business decisions that were not previously possible. By executing predictive or advanced analytics directly in a database, users can perform critical drill-downs and deep analyses that were previously not possible or practical. In addition, the in-database approach allows businesses to analyze big data faster, more accurately, and more cost-effectively than ever before in even the most complex, data-intensive environments.

Innovative and leading-edge organizations have realized that effective use of analytics enables them to outperform their peers and improve key processes such as customer targeting and retention, product development, pricing, risk assessment and management, marketing, and sales. It has become a motto that the more advanced your analytical capabilities are, the better equipped you will be to construct and fine-tune successful business strategies for data-driven decisions. These data-driven decisions will increase productivity, efficiency, the bottom line, and even brand value.

This means that, for example, a telecommunications organization can conduct more thorough and meticulous churn analysis and create optimal pricing programs. Insurance companies can run more effective exposure assessments, improve fraud detection, and develop targeted customer retention programs. Financial institutions can enhance their ongoing portfolio analysis activities, upsell customers with new products or offerings, better mitigate risk, and increase individual customer profitability. Marketers in virtually every industry can conduct real-time campaign analysis, enabling them to tweak or abandon campaigns in order to maximize returns on their marketing spend.

From C-level executives to line-of-business managers and frontline employees in sales, service, finance, marketing and other disciplines, leveraging in-database analytics will improve performance, productivity, innovation, and overall competitive advantage.

SUCCESS STORIES AND USE CASES

There are a number of success stories and use cases for in-database analytics since its inception into the industry. As previously mentioned, in-database analytics is used to explore the data, prepare the data for analysis, and develop and deploy the model. Let's examine some success stories and use cases for in-database processing.

E-Commerce: Data Preparation and Data Processing

Our first success story comes from a multinational corporation and e-commerce company that provides consumer-to-consumer and business-to-consumer sales services via the Internet. This corporation leverages in-database processing to prepare the data and increase end-to-end performance.

With a very sophisticated and large data management system, there is also an extensive analytic ecosystem analyzing the petabytes of data stored in the data platform. Their data platform is used to discover, explore, analyze, and report the data using various analytics tools. Figure 2.3 shows data integration, data platform, and data analytics.

The data platform is where in-database processing will be executed. In Figure 2.3, the data platform builds a strong foundation for analytics and has structured and semi-structured data consisting of transactions and web logs of 36 petabytes of customer and behavior data. Analyzing millions of rows and hundreds of columns of data within a finite time frame with the traditional approach presented many constraints. These included transferring large amounts of data, managing massive storage space with duplicated data, and administering

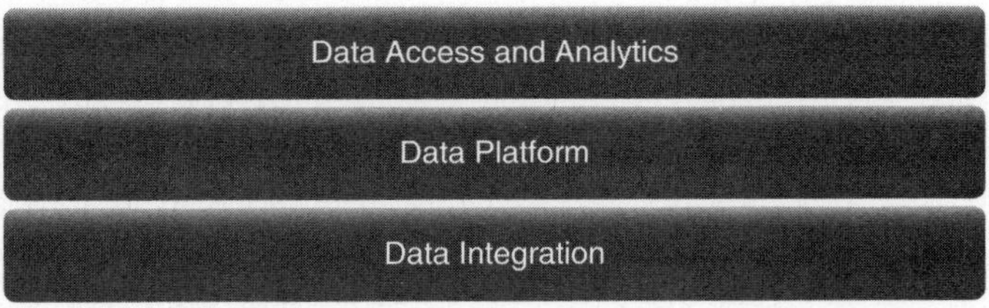

Figure 2.3 Data and analytic ecosystem

system resources. In addition, the volume and frequency of data to be processed has opened up several challenges around data preparation and transformation, data transfer between the data platform and data access and analytics, data set storage, and optimum system resource utilization, leading to increased data set processing costs and scalability bottlenecks. Due to the limitations with the traditional approach and infrastructure, the customer decided to adopt in-database technologies for the flexibility and efficient way in which to analyze the increasing amounts of data being collected. By integrating analytics into the database or data warehouse and applying the analytics to where the data reside, it is able to scale and provide better performance compared to the current approach and infrastructure. By moving data preparation, analytics, and reporting tasks to where the data are offers many benefits such as increasing speed and performance, reducing data movement, and promoting enhanced data governance for the IT department. For decision makers, the in-database approach provides faster access to the analytical results, which lead to more agile and accurate data-driven decisions. Let's examine the before-and-after picture and the benefits of in-database processing.

Figure 2.4 provides a look at the traditional approach to analyzing customer behavior from summarized tables processed on a daily basis. The process involves creating a data set from an underlying summarized table from the data warehouse. It consists of four major steps, all triggered by a wrapper script. In the first step, the parameters necessary for analysis are entered into a text file (parameter source file) as macro variables. Then, a sequence of SQLs on the database is executed, which yields a summarized table in the data warehouse. This table acts as the source data for all the subsequent processes. In the next step, a program uses fast-export process with multiple sessions to transfer the table from the data warehouse onto the analytics server and a data set created. The analysis is then performed on this data set to provide test analysis at different dimensions based on multiple aggregations. The output after analysis of each dimension is appended to the final output data set. The final step transfers the results back from the analytical data set to table in the data warehouse using fast-load process. This result or output from the data set is visualized on different dashboards by using a visualization or business intelligence tool for end-user consumption.

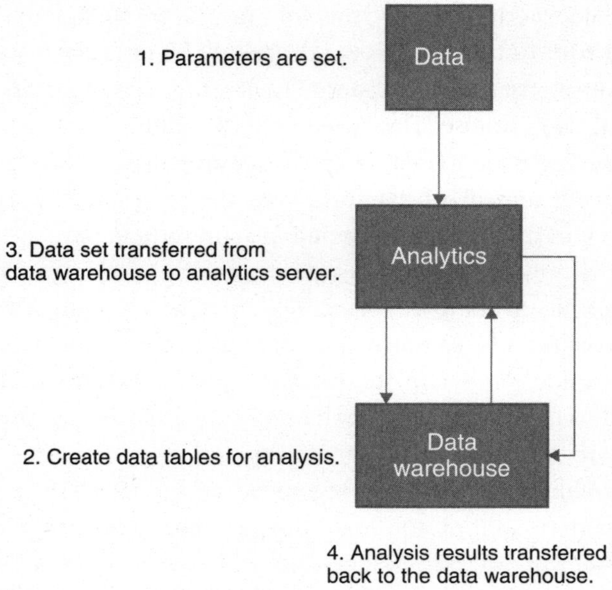

Figure 2.4 Traditional approach

Table 2.1 Traditional Run Times at Different Process

Process	Description	Time (Minutes)
SQL running on the data warehouse	Create a table from the data warehouse to be analyzed in the analytics server	32
Data transfer (data warehouse to analytics server)	Transfer of table from data warehouse to analytical data set using fast export utility	52
Statistical computation	Processing of data at different dimensions	233
Data transfer (analytics to data warehouse)	Transfer of output data set to data warehouse	6
		Total: 323 minutes

Table 2.1 illustrates the process and time for each step in the traditional approach. A typical test analysis usually consists of over 200 million records with over 100 variables of customer behavior.

Table 2.1 clearly shows that the SQL step takes around 30 minutes to create a summarized table from the data warehouse. Data transfer from the data warehouse to be used in the analytics server usually takes almost an hour to transfer the data. Looking forward, as the data volume increases, the processing time will increase proportionally and is scalable for this purpose. The analysis is provided for different dimensions of the data set. The data set is aggregated multiple times, and analysis is performed on the summary data set created after aggregation. This part of statistical computation takes around four hours, which is the bulk of the total processing time. The final transfer from output data set to the data warehouse is about six minutes. On the whole, the standard process consumed around five hours, which is too time consuming and resource intensive to maintain. In addition, any "tweaks" or changes to the process will take several business days to test and implement.

There are several challenges with the traditional process. First and foremost, this process uses fast export approach with multiple sessions, and this might take a lot of bandwidth on the server. In addition, the data transfer may fail if the volume of data is massive and the process has to be restarted. More system resources are needed to process such volume of data, so there is a limitation to execute only one or two processes at a time. This will put restrictions on the whole process to perform the analysis in a tight time frame.

In-Database Process

Now let's examine the effects of leveraging in-database technology in this process. Table 2.2 compares the processing time between the traditional and in-database approach.

With the in-database processing, the transfer phase of data from the data warehouse to the analytical server is eliminated, which decreases the processing time by almost one hour. Statistical computation takes around 45 minutes as aggregation of data is pushed to database side and summary data set is created, which acts as a source to further processing. The final transfer from the analytical data set to the data warehouse is around 6 minutes. On the whole, in-database process is 83 minutes.

The initial step of running SQLs on the database is similar in both processes as it takes around 32 minutes. The data transfer part is

Table 2.2 In-Database Run Times at Different Process

Process	Description	Time (minutes) Traditional Approach	Time (Minutes) In-Database
SQL running on the data warehouse	Create a table from the data warehouse to be analyzed in the analytics server	32	32
Data transfer (data warehouse to analytics server)	Transfer of table from data warehouse to analytical data set using fast export utility	52	0
Statistical computation	Processing of data at different dimensions	233	45
Data transfer (analytics output to data warehouse)	Transfer of output data set to data warehouse table	6	6
		Total: 323 minutes	83 minutes

completely eliminated for in-database process compared to standard process, as aggregations are performed in the database as against the analytic server. The run time taken for statistical computation has drastically reduced for in-database process compared to standard process. This is a major improvement to the traditional process and the way analytics is executed. This is achieved by using in-database processing which converts analytical pocedures to SQL. The SQL code is executed on the database, aggregating the data warehouse table multiple times by taking advantage of a highly optimized, massively parallel processing system and performing the functions in parallel. On the other hand, in standard process, the data are transferred from data warehouse table to analytical data set, and aggregations are performed on this analytical data set. The final step remains the same in both the processes, wherein analytical data set is loaded back into the data warehouse table. In the traditional process, it takes 323 minutes; the in-database approach reduces that time to 83 minutes—a fourfold increase in performance.

This process decreases the end-to-end processing times while increasing the processing throughput. There has been an overall reduction in system resource utilization that allows for a greater degree of parallelism and performance. There has been a dramatic reduction in disk space utilization by not having to store data on the analytics server. As the processing time has reduced, additional insights and analyses were provided for all the tests without major increase in the run time. The process also consumed less data transfer bandwidth on both the servers (analytics and data warehouse) and on the network, so other processes were able to take advantage of the servers and enhance data governance. Finally, it is less prone to issues such as timed-out sessions and terminations.

Advantages of in-database processing

- Decreasing processing time by a factor of four
- Eliminating of input and output costs as there is no transfer of data
- Summarizing large amounts of data on DBMS side, which is faster, as most of them are highly optimized, scalable, and tuned
- Enabling analytic functions directly to the data
- Increasing throughput by reducing in system resource utilization and allowing for greater degree of parallelism
- Increasing performance and eliminating data movement
- Optimizing resource utilization across an integrated analytic/warehousing environment
- Improving data quality and integrity
- Reducing network traffic
- Enhancing the effectiveness of analysts, who can stay focused on higher-value tasks
- Lowering the total cost of ownership/increasing return on investment

This e-commerce company continues to use in-database processing on a daily basis. One of the feedbacks they shared at this point in time is that not all of the analytical functions that they use are enabled in-database. Some processing continues to run in the traditional process. In-database is great when it is available to be executed, but it is also complementary to the overall analytical architecture.

Future Direction

This e-commerce customer continues to use in-database analytics. It is planning to expand the use of in-database analytics to other departments and is exploring the integration with Hadoop. As data volumes continue to grow, the company is adding more capacity to manage the enterprise data warehouse and complement the in-database analytics to prepare and explore various types of data.

Telecommunication: Developing a Data Model Using In-Database Technology

In our next success story and use case, we have a customer based in Europe. This company is one of the largest telecommunication carriers in Central Europe. With the company earnings under pressure due to falling prices, declining customer loyalty, and competitive nature, there is an enormous need to understand customer behavior in order to diminish the rising churn rates.

Churn analysis is important in every industry, but particularly in the telecommunication sector. Churn analysis is the process of identifying potential defectors and determining the causal factors, so that the company can try to prevent the attrition from happening in the future. Every telecommunication provider uses churn prediction to segment early warning for customer retention and marketing analysis. Segment early warning would be an application of churn analysis in campaign management. It basically is a combination of customer churn segmentation and customer value segmentation. The resulting subsegments (e.g., highest-value customer with neutral churn risk between 30% and 70%) are used for differentiated retention offers to the customer base and help to reduce overall costs of customer retention. Building an effective churn analysis relies heavily on granular customer data, which consists of large amounts of data and a variety of data sources.

One of the key aspects in churn analysis is to minimize modeling latency so that timely reactions can be taken due to market changes. To complete the end-to-end analysis, an automated scoring process should be included in order to have churn scores available on an hourly, daily, or weekly data. At the same time, to take advantage of granular and large amounts usage data in the form of call detail records and in order to optimize this churn model, it needs to have a well and tightly integrated data warehousing and analytics environment to minimize any type of latency between the environments, which historically have been only loosely integrated for this organization.

Background

Working with the customer, this organization started with a business background and a well-defined business problem. In the business background, we learned that the analysts work closely with business representatives, for example, from organizational groups like segment management or a retention office, to formulate the analytical "problem" at hand. The analyst begins the model-building process, typically starting with gathering and preparing the data (statistical data preparation) for their needs before actually developing and validating the model. Once the analyst settles on a model that they deem most sufficient to predict customer churn and satisfy the business problem, this model will have to be deployed to an automated and governed IT process for the recurring scoring of new data sources.

The following will explain how in-database processing and analytics can be applied in the various phases of this model-building process to predict and execute customer churn.

Creating a Data Set

The most essential component of information is the customer level analytical data set. A single data record in this data set is also referred to as the customer analytic record. A series of data preparation steps are usually required to create this record-level analytical data set. The data includes contract information, customer contact information, recharging for prepaid, customer life value, and other behavioral characteristics including service usage. Behavioral information can be found in the call detail records. Such usage information, gathered and transformed on a record-level for each customer entity, typically includes the number of calls or minutes of use, ratio of week-days versus week-end calls, or similar metrics. The granular call detail records data on call level are typically aggregated up to a weekly or monthly granularity before used in model development.

The behavioral data aggregated from call detail records are combined with contract, recharging, and customer contact data. Everything is available in full history and detail on the data warehouse. The aggregation and combination steps are executed directly in the data warehouse, comprising several hundreds of attributes ready to be used in churn modeling. The combination of data is typically implemented as joins, sorts, and merges within the data warehouse.

One best practice is to make aware of the resulting analytic data set at the data warehouse level. This means ensuring that all relevant changes of customer behavior are traced and recorded and that proper timestamps are assigned to these changes. Generally, this process is a prerequisite to achieving the goal of establishing the data warehouse as a corporate repository. In this case, all behaviors related to the customers are pursued over a certain time and are used for the actual modeling to develop a churn model.

Data Exploration

Before building the analytical data set, the analytic user would work against tables in a customer database, either a stand-alone data model or a domain within an enterprise data model inside the database or data warehouse, for all customers in the active population. Based on the understanding of the source data, the analytic user would then move to the next step, building the analytical data set as input for developing the analytic model.

By using the in-database functions such as summary, frequency, and means, the analyst will further explore the analytical data set at this stage to understand the behavior of attributes across subscriptions or groups of customers within the population to identify the expected behavior but also unexpected patterns in subgroups—especially by using the frequency analysis with stratified analysis by computing statistics across the analytical data set as well as within churner versus nonchurner groups of subscriptions. Summary, means, and frequency all compute descriptive statistics for variables across all customer records.

Data Preparation

After having explored the source data for mediated call data, billing data, and recharging data, we can now transform this source data to the customer analytic records at subscription level granularity, with calling, information about a customer recharging his phone, and many more attributes for model development; for example, there can be multiple subscriptions for a single customer. For churn-prediction modeling activities, the analytic data set captures active subscription customer analytic records as well as churned subscription customer analytic records.

In the data preparation step, the analyst will use the customer or related subscription behavior derived from the analytical data set to refine existing attributes or generate additional attributes into the analytic data set using statistical derivations. A good example is principal component analysis (PCA) techniques using the in-database principal components procedure. Depending on research objectives, a similar technique would be a factor analysis, also available as in-database factor function.

One mathematical technique used in this churn analysis is combining variables into factors and reducing the number of variables under consideration in order to obtain the most information about the customers and develop an effective data model.

A typical application in churn-prediction modeling would be to reduce a group of usage behavior attributes (e.g., 3 months, 6 months, 12 months average number of calls) with factor analysis. As a result, we can use a reduced number of attributes for modeling, which has a number of advantages (statistical and practical ones) over using a larger number of attributes.

Alternatively, the modeler can use the in-database capable variable selection procedure to run through this step in a more automated fashion. Many data-mining databases have hundreds and thousands of potential inputs which are model attributes. The variable selection procedure allows quick identification of input variables that are useful for predicting the target variables based on a linear models framework.

Model Development

There are several data-mining methodologies on the market that are recommended sources for more process-specific details. In this section, we will focus on demonstrating how the in-database technology can be applied in the model-development process.

Logistic regression is a robust method, and we see it very often used for building churn-prediction models. To be used by logistic regression analysis, a certain number of churned lines are combined with a number of lines still active in order to prepare modeling.

The analyst can use the in-database procedures such as linear and logistic regression analysis. Linear regression attempts to predict the value of a continuous target as a linear function of one or more independent inputs. Logistic regression attempts to predict the probability that a categorical (binary, ordinal, or nominal) target will acquire the event of interest as a function of one or more independent inputs.

In our example of churn prediction modeling, the logistic regression will be used when a categorical target attribute is used (note that this is the predominant case). The function supports forward, backward, and stepwise selection methods. It also allows the scoring of a data set.

The regression procedure computes a model in which the dependent churn target variable is modeled as a linear equation of multiple independent variables by a least squares function. We might consider REG, for example, when we decide to define the churn target attribute as percentage decrease in usage. The REG procedure has numerous model-fitting options, which include many model selection variations and hypothesis tests. Regression analysis is often used to identify a subset of independent variables that have unique and significant relationships with the dependent variable. In this case, the REG procedure is used for its exploratory analysis, in addition to its extensive model fitting and reporting functions.

As a result of this core model development step, the analyst defines the churn prediction model to be deployed for regular scoring of newly incoming data inside the database.

Model Deployment

In-database scoring is used in the deployment step of the churn prediction modeling. Deployment of models in the customer retention business process requires recurrent scoring of the active subscriber base with the selected churn model.

The scoring function produces churn scores per subscription in the form of a table in the data warehouse that contains predicted churn risk and/or residuals from a model that is estimated using the regression procedure in-database. The in-database scoring function dynamically generates SQL code for the given model. This function then submits the SQL code to the database, which produces a table without having to extract any rows of data.

Table 2.3 is a summary of value and benefits using in-database technology achieved from the telecommunication company.

Table 2.3 Benefits of In-Database Processing

Capability	Value
Streamline analytic workflow	▪ Accelerate data discovery ▪ Minimize data preparation ▪ Decrease time to value
Scalability and performance	▪ Reduce data movement ▪ Leverage the database for parallelization
Data consistency	▪ Reduce data redundancy ▪ Reduce information latency
Fit for IT	▪ Enable data governance ▪ Increase hardware utilization ▪ Integrate with resource management ▪ Facilitate standardization on a single enterprise analytics platform
Productivity	▪ Increase business user productivity ▪ Minimize network traffic ▪ Provide high quality analytical data models

In addition, the customer shared these positive impacts on the business:

- Receives an early warning when customer behavior changes, enabling fast reaction with new offers.
- Improves customer retention and the bottom line. Sales people can bring up all relevant data on screen while talking to a customer.
- Isolates high churn rate in a customer's geographical or social network neighborhood, which leads to proactive propagation and marketing campaigns.
- Expands line of business into other markets by executing cross-sell promotions into other markets.

Churn analysis is applicable in every industry, but more so in the telecommunication industry due to its highly competitive nature and plethora of options for consumers. By having the right technology and infrastructure, this telecommunication company was able to turn around its declining business and ultimately be proactive by responding to customer behavior, instead of just reacting when it is too late. To borrow a quote from Bill Gates, "Your most unhappy customers are your greatest source of learning."[1]

Financial: In-Database Model Development and Deployment

A major European financial organization identified that its cycle time from model initiation to model deployment was unsatisfactory with the changes in a global, competitive economy. The process was manual, error-prone, and resource-intensive. The process had little or no monitoring to identify model degradation.

This organization developed a flexible and efficient infrastructure for flexible data management, model development, and model deployment using in-database technology. The platform harnesses the power of the database environment for data preparation and model scoring and uses the power of analytics to build the complex and

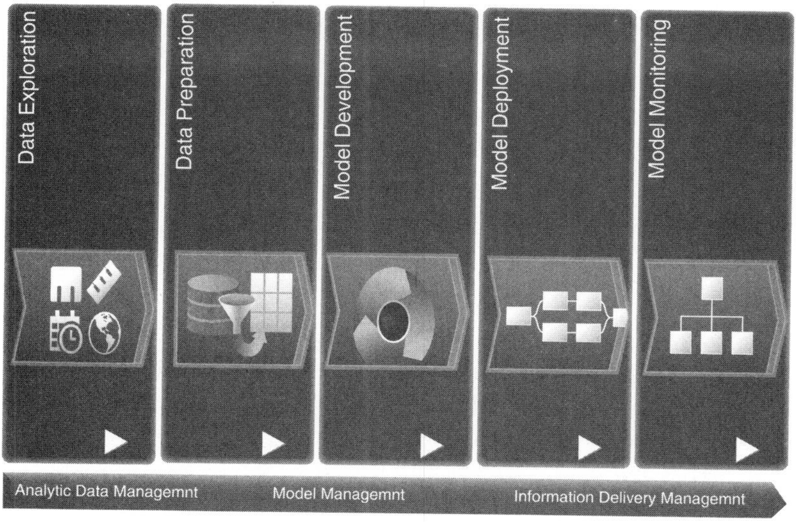

Figure 2.5 In-database process

comprehensive analytical data models. By leveraging the massively parallel power of the database, over 55 million records can be scored within the database many times during the day. This could not have been accomplished with the older and traditional process. Figure 2.5 shows the process that this customer has implemented within its organization.

By adopting the in-database processing, the numerous months that it usually took for a model to be promoted to a production environment were dramatically reduced down to days. There was a 40 percent reduction in data preparation, and analysts are 50 percent more productive doing more strategic initiatives. This financial company was able to increase performance, economics, and governance.

Let's examine how this financial institution was able to apply analytics and the challenges they encountered.

Challenges with the Traditional Approach

Due to the competitive nature of the financial industry and the evolving needs of their valued customers, the traditional approach was not meeting their needs to maintain a competitive advantage and leadership in their market. The top three challenges that this institution faces are common to many other organizations:

Manual process

The steps to prepare the data and build a data model require multiple areas of the business to be involved. In a typical project an analyst is required to build the model, an IT team executes and deploys the model, then a database administrator centrally manages the data warehouse. As each business area hands off the results to another area, there is a delay. Each area has to check and validate what has happened to the model and data. In many areas, it is common that a model is recoded from one language to another. There might be many iterations of the model before the best model is ready. Because of so much manual involvement, incorrectly coded models can be deployed into a production environment that leads to incorrect results, which could have devastating consequences.

Data governance

In the traditional approach, data sources are scattered across the organization, and the data use for model development is not in the right format. Analysts tend to massage that data by creating their own analytical data mart or data silo. In addition, they generate additional summarizations of the data. All of these data preparation methods lead to inconsistent data, with different versions of data used to build the model. As a result, the data in the model development environment are inconsistent and may lead to different results. Since the data are distributed, some are kept on file servers and some on mapped drives, and, in extreme cases, some data are on local hard drives. This causes major issues with data governance because there are so many silos of data. Data on local hard drives results in processing on the desktop, which can mean poor performance.

Disjointed technologies

Data in a data warehouse are used by many different analytical teams, which may result in multiple copies of data and locations. All of these duplicates lead to multiple storage and large data transfers across networks. Needless to say, analysts might use different analytical software to develop the models. When it is time to promote the model to a production environment, analysts may have to translate the mode or recode into a common standard. Models degrade over time, so they must be constantly monitored and managed. Model monitoring in the production environment is not consistent because different spreadsheets can be used to monitor the model. Models degrade over time, so they must be constantly monitored and managed. Because different technologies are being leveraged at different stages and none of them are integrated, it can deliver inconsistent models and outputs.

In-Database Approach

To mitigate the risks and challenges just described, the customer conducted a proof of concept with in-database technologies and saw immediate value from the readout. The customer saw that in-database processing takes advantages of the massively parallel processing (MPP) architecture of the database or data warehouse for scalability and better performance. Moving data management and analytics to where the data reside is beneficial in terms of speed and performance. This move reduces other unnecessary data moves and promotes greater data governance.

Data preparation

The data warehouse provides the primary source of data for analysis. An ETL tool is used to extract, load, and transform (ELT) data that produce the analytical data set. During the extraction phase, a data source or system is accessed, and only the data that is needed is obtained. The data are then staged in the data warehouse using high-speed connectors to ensure that the data are loaded quickly. The data are transformed into a structure that is fit for model development.

Model development

Developing an analytical data model is often performed by an analyst. The modeler provides various options that automatically treat the data to handle many scenarios such as outliers, missing values, rare target events, skewed data, correlated variables, variable selection, and model building and selection. When model development is complete, analysts register a model package centrally in metadata. A model package contains all of the scoring code that is needed when the model is deployed. It contains optimized scoring code that includes only the necessary transformations from the scoring code, eliminating any transformations that are redundant.

The model package contains information about the name of the algorithm that was used, the name of the data-mining analyst, and the time of creation. This is useful information for data governance. A model package is associated with a project. This enables the model deployment team to see the model that has been built by the analyst and all of the associated output. A review of the model ensures that the right steps have been taken and a suitable and robust model is released into the production environment.

Model deployment

Once a model has been reviewed, signed off, and declared ready for production, it is considered champion status. The model is converted into a vendor-defined function and then placed in the data warehouse. A vendor-defined function is a database-specific function that contains all of the scoring logic that is required for a model to run. By placing the vendor defined function in the data warehouse, security, auditing, and administration can be applied and leveraged.

The model can now be scored. The scoring process can take place in-database and is scheduled to run at a specific time interval, or when it is initiated by a trigger.

Model monitoring and retirement

Once a model is in a production environment, and is being executed at regular intervals, the model is centrally monitored because its predictive performance will degrade over time. You can use a model manager tool to view a variety of monitoring reports that have been created. The model can be retired when its performance degradation hits a certain threshold, and it can be replaced with a new model that has been recalibrated or rebuilt. Over time, the mode needs to be recalibrated or redeveloped.

Benefits of Using In-Database Processing

In addition to the increased productivity as indicated previously, this financial company experienced many other value-added benefits with in-database processing. Following is a list of tangible and intangible benefits gained from using in-database technologies:

- Reducing model development time since data are integrated and consistent.
- Decreasing deployment time because the scoring code needs no conversion. This eliminates the timely and error-prone manual process of translating the model.
- Faster-scoring processes since the model can be scored in the database, which leverages the scalability and processing speed offered in the database. This reduces scoring times from hours and days to minutes and seconds.
- Minimizing risk by using consistent processes and integrated technologies for model development and deployment.

The customer successfully focused its efforts and attention to the core of analytics—which is the model development and deployment. Now, I want to draw your attention to a topic—data quality—which is near and dear to my profession. Without addressing data quality, the analyses and results can be misleading and deliver incorrect insights for making business decisions.

IN-DATABASE DATA QUALITY

The adage "garbage in, garbage out" becomes an unfortunate reality when data quality is not addressed. This is the information age, and we base our decisions on insights gained from data. If inaccurate data are entered without subsequent data quality checks, only inaccurate information will prevail. Bad data can affect businesses in varying degrees, ranging from simple misrepresentation of information to multimillion-dollar mistakes.

In fact, numerous research and studies have concluded that data quality is the culprit behind many failed data warehousing and analytics projects. With the large price tags on these high-profile initiatives and the importance of accurate information to business analytics, improving data quality has become a top management priority.

With big data, you now have to store and manage large amounts of data that need to be cleansed and integrated. By integrating data management and data quality, a consistent, reliable view of your organization ensures that critical decisions are based only on accurate information with in-database data quality. If you trust your data, you can trust your decisions with in-database data quality.

Background

According to a Gartner report titled "Measuring the Business Value of Data Quality", 40% of business initiatives fail due to poor data quality. Big data warehousing and analytics projects have failed due to data quality issues. The Data Warehousing Institute reports that billions and billions of dollars are lost because of poor data quality.[2] The cost accounts only for U.S. business losses in postage, printing, and staffing overhead. Frighteningly, the real cost of poor data quality is much higher. Beyond wasted resources, there are disgruntled customers, decreases in sales revenues, erosion of credibility, and the inability to make sound business decisions. Sometimes the effects of bad data cause enough damage for complete business failure.

Organizations depend on data. Regardless of the industry, revenue size, or the market it serves, every organization relies on its data to produce useful information for effective business decision making. Unfortunately, with so much emphasis on such information, data quality rarely gets the attention it deserves. No one wants to consciously admit that business decisions are based on inaccurate or incomplete data. TDWI revealed that 75 percent of organizations have no data quality processes in place.[3] It appears that the majority of the businesses have taken no steps to determine the severity of data quality issues and its impact on the bottom line.

Companies invest hundreds of thousands of dollars and significantly large portions of information technology (IT) budgets on building sophisticated databases and data warehouses. In the quest for successful business intelligence, various applications and systems will be deployed and information gathering processes will be created. However, many overlook the essential fact that it is the underlying data that matters. All of the fantastic screens and reports in the world will not make a positive difference if the data that supports the system is inconsistent, redundant, and full of errors.

There are many reasons why the quality of the data that companies collect and analyze is so poor. The reasons vary everything from the very ambiguous nature of the data itself to the reliance on data entry perfection. But none is more compelling than the simple fact that companies rely on so many different data sources to obtain a holistic view of the business.

Information collection is increasing more than tenfold each year, with the Internet a major driver in this trend. As more and more data are collected, the reality of a multi-channel world that includes e-business, direct sales, call centers, and existing systems sets in. Bad data (i.e., inconsistent, incomplete, duplicate, or redundant data) are affecting companies at an alarming rate, and the dilemma is how to optimize the use of corporate data within every application, system, and database throughout the enterprise.

Take into consideration the director of data warehousing at a major electronic component manufacturer who realized there was a problem linking information between an inventory database and a customer order database. The inventory database had data fields that represented product numbers differently than the customer order database. Nothing was done about it. There were hundreds of thousands of records that would have to be reviewed and changed but there were no resources available to take on this tremendous, time-consuming task. As a result, more than 500 customer orders were unfulfilled. At an average order per customer of $5000, the resulting loss of US$2.5 million in revenue was significant.

Data Quality Defined

Data quality is often defined as a process of arranging information so that individual records are accurate, updated, and consistently represented. Accurate information relies on clean and consistent data that usually includes names, addresses, email addresses, phone numbers, and so on. Good data quality means that an organization's data are accurate, complete, consistent, timely, unique, and valid. The better the data, the more clearly it presents an accurate, consolidated view of the organization, across systems, departments, and line of businesses.

Technological advancements that use data pattern analysis, *smart clustering,* numerous data algorithms, and a host of other sophisticated capabilities ensure that data gathered throughout the organization is accurate, usable, and consistent. By intelligently identifying, standardizing, correcting, matching, and consolidating data, software solutions offer much needed relief to organizational data quality headaches.

Today organizations are looking for a wide range of features in data quality tools. According to the report by TDWI, standardization and verification top the list of desired capabilities, followed by tools that define and validate business rules. Other important features include matching, consolidation, and integration with other enterprise applications such as analytics.

Business Challenges

Bad data originates from a variety of sources—errors in data entry, erroneous data received from Internet forms, faulty data purchased or acquired from an outside source, or simply combining good data with outdated data and not having the ability to distinguish between the two.

One obstacle to creating good data is simply examining what is available and developing a plan for how it will be used. You will need to determine which data are good, which are bad, and how bad the bad data are. Most organizations have little or no idea about the quality of the data residing in their systems and applications.

According to TDWI, almost half (44 percent) of the respondents said the quality of the data within their companies was "worse than everyone thinks."[4] This same report chronicles examples of costs and missed opportunities due to inaccurate or incomplete data:

- A telecommunications firm lost $8 million a month because data entry errors incorrectly coded accounts, preventing bills from being sent out.
- An insurance company lost hundreds of thousands of dollars annually in mailing costs (postage, returns, collateral, and staff to process returns) due to duplicate customer and prospect records.
- A global chemical company discovered it was losing millions of dollars in volume discounts in procuring supplies because it could not correctly identify and reconcile suppliers on a global basis.

Sadly, most companies are oblivious to the true business impact of poor quality data. The simple truth is that poor data quality absolutely affects the bottom line. Accurate, complete data reduces costs in a number of ways, from the simple and obvious marketing savings (postage and production costs on a direct marketing piece, for example) to the less obvious organizational efficiency savings.

According to the same Data Quality Survey (mentioned earlier), almost half of the surveyed companies suffered losses, problems, or costs due to poor quality data. Companies also cited extra costs due to duplicate mailings, excess inventory, inaccurate billing, and lost discounts, as well as customer dissatisfaction, delays in deploying new systems, and loss of revenue.

Data as a Strategic Asset

Data should be treated as a key strategic asset, so ensuring its quality is imperative. Organizations collect data from various sources: legacy, databases, external providers, the Web, and so on. Due to the tremendous amount of data variety and sources, quality is often compromised. It is a common problem that many organizations are reluctant to admit and address. The single most challenging aspect for companies is to recognize and determine the severity of their data quality issues and face the problem head-on to obtain resolution. Spending the money, time, and resources to collect massive volumes of data without ensuring the quality of the data is futile and only leads to disappointment.

Cleansing data at the source is a significant way to enhance the success of a data warehouse and analytics. Thus, it becomes a proactive rather than reactive model. Simply collecting data is no longer sufficient. It is more important to make proper sense of the data and to ensure its accuracy. As the amount of data escalates, so does the amount of inaccurate information obtained from the data. Data should be cleansed at the source in order to detect and address problems early in the process so that quality issues are prevented further down the line.

Information is all about integration and interaction of data points. Inaccuracies in a single data column can ultimately affect the results and may directly affect the cost of doing business and the quality of business decisions. Preventive measures to ensure data quality usually are more economical and less painful. Delaying the inevitable data cleansing dramatically increases the cost of doing so, as well as increases how long the cleansing process takes to complete.

Improved synergy between the extraction, loading, and transformation (ETL) warehousing process and data quality offers the ability to more easily manage complex data integration. By applying data quality in the ETL process, data integrity and accuracy are assured. Much of the data warehousing effort is concentrated in the ETL process with the extraction of records and fields from various data sources, conversion of the data to new formats, and the loading of data to other target destinations such as a warehouse or a data mart. The purpose of the ETL process is to load the warehouse with integrated and cleansed data. Data quality focuses on the contents of the individual records to ensure the data loaded into the target destination are accurate, reliable, and consistent.

The Value of In-Database Data Quality

The technology for in-database data quality has only been on the market for about three years. Not many vendors offer this capability. This technology is neither as mature nor as advanced as in-database analytics. Enabling in-database data quality provides value to both business analysts and IT professionals. Many of the IT professionals focus heavily on the ETL process since its purpose is to load the data warehouse with integrated and cleansed data. However, data quality is a key component in the preparation for entry into the data warehouse. The best place to clean the data is in the source system so the defects cannot extend to the data warehouse and other interrelated systems. There are several methods and processes to achieve integrated and cleansed data.

Data Auditing and Standardization

One of the most popular data quality processes is standardizing the data. Now, you can standardize the data in-database. Data in a database or data store typically are inconsistent and lack conformity. There are many ways to say the same thing. As Table 2.4 illustrates, a title may be expressed in various ways.

If a direct mailing campaign plans to extract 5,000 "VP of Sales" out of a database by writing a query, and the query does not include every possible way that "vice president of sales" is represented, then the search will miss some of the target names. Inconsistently represented data are more difficult to aggregate or query. If the data are not represented consistently, it is even more difficult to perform any meaningful analysis of the data.

The first step in the cleansing process is data auditing. Data auditing provides counts and frequencies for data fields. It also identifies unique values and range reports with maximum and minimum values. In this phase, you should also define your business and cleansing rules. Once you have analyzed the values, then you can standardize the title for consistency.

Table 2.4 Variations of Title

Name	Title
Jane Doe1	VP of Sales
Jane Doe2	Vice President of Sales
Jane Doe3	V.P. of Sales
Jane Doe4	Vice Pres. of Sales

Data Consolidation and Matching Analysis

Another important data-quality process is matching and consolidating records. Anyone who gets two or three of the same advertisement or magazine instead of a single copy to which you subscribed is likely experiencing a perfect example of a "duplicate record" problem in the customer database. In some cases, there are probably small variations in the way the subscriber's name or address appear in the database. Table 2.5 illustrates the example.

William Doe may have several contact points and enter various kinds of contact information. A human being would look at these variations and instantly recognize that these names represent the same person, but a computer would store these as different records—hence multiple copies of the same advertisement or magazine. In this case, resources are allocated on inaccurate information extracted and loaded into the data warehouse with duplicate or redundant data. This problem can obviously be very costly for any organization that routinely mails against a large customer database.

Data consolidation and matching analysis are fundamental to the data management and data quality process. These capabilities link data from multiple sources and identify records that represent the same individual, company, or entity. The process of consolidation combines the elements of identifying matching records into a single, complete record (often called the golden or master record).

Matching and standardizing routines are necessary to analyze, cleanse, and consolidate data from a variety of platforms and sources. It includes defect analysis and corrections for invalid data and data authentication processes.

Table 2.5 Duplicate Records

Name	Address	Country
William Doe	900 Sunset Dr	USA
Will Doe	900 Sun set Dr.	U.S.A
Bill Doe	900 Sunset Drive	US
Billy Doe	900 Sunset	United States
Mr. W. N. Doe	900 SunSet Drive	U.S.

Other In-Database Data Quality Functions

Standardizing and matching of data are the most prevalent data quality functions, and they are most useful in-database. Other in-database functions include:

- *Casing*: Ensures context-appropriate casing is used in a data column.
- *Extraction*: Extracts context-specific entities or attributes from text string.
- *Gender analysis*: Determines the gender of a name.
- *Identification analysis*: Determines the type of data represented by a text string.
- *Parsing*: Segments a string into separate, discrete entities.
- *Pattern analysis*: Shows simple representation of a text string's character pattern. It's useful to determine if further data quality processing is necessary.

As in-database data quality evolves and customers are demanding more in-database data-quality functions, I truly believe it is an essential element to conquering big data and analytics.

Value of In-Database Data Quality

Like in-database analytics, in-database data quality offers valuable benefits and advantages. Imagine what you can accomplish when data quality processes you once considered too complex are not only possible, but can be done quickly and with minimal effort. You will get your big data under control in no time—which leads to big ideas. It has big potential and possibly an even bigger payoff.

With in-database data quality, you can:

- Become more agile, reacting with lightning speed to new opportunities and challenges.
- Improve productivity by minimizing time spent on moving and manipulating data.
- Boost security by keeping data intact and in a single, highly governed environment.

- Seamlessly manage the flow of cleansed data throughout the enterprise.
- Keep costs in check by using an integrated solution instead of piecemeal technology.

It is a fact that ignoring data quality is costly, and it affects every industry that relies on accurate and consistent information. Data quality is a continuous process and effort. By addressing data quality at the source, data cleansing becomes a proactive rather than a reactive process. The integration of data quality with the database minimizes the risk of failure, cost, and number of resources to manage the data. The synergy between ETL and data quality provides integrated and cleansed data for your warehouse, mart, or other repository. Data are a vital resource and should be treated as a key strategic asset in order to obtain reliable and accurate view of your organization.

INVESTMENT FOR IN-DATABASE PROCESSING

Customers often express interest for in-database processing, but they are concerned? about the investment or costs to adopt and implement this technology. I frequently tell customers and prospects that it will require some investment in software, hardware, and training the staff to a new process. There are a handful of analytic vendors that are working closely with the database vendors to deliver in-database processing.

From the software perspective, the analytic marketplace varies—open source, small boutique start-ups, visionary, market leaders. The open source vendors are starting to integrate with some of the database vendors to offer cost-effective in-database solutions with a lower total cost of ownership. With open source, there is a large and growing user community to leverage for sample code and implementation approach. However, it can be limited to analyzing large data volumes because it is memory bound and is single-threaded processing for constrained performance. Niche or small-boutique analytic vendors are also entering the in-database solutions. They offer another low-cost alternative with more modern user interface for those who prefer the nontraditional manual coding technique. On the other hand, users may not have the depth and breadth of analytic capabilities and may not be certified as a standard in industries such as health care, finance, or pharmaceutical. Finally, the visionaries or leaders in analytics offer the most robust and mature in-database solutions. Not only do they offer the depth and breadth of in-database functions, but they also deliver many proven methodologies, integrated consulting services, and documented best practices. Users can easily adopt these solutions with minimal changes to their existing code or process to applying in-database.

As the name implies, in-database processing would require the database vendors to deliver the hardware and software for the database to host the data for analytics. Unlike the analytics market space, most of the database vendors that offer in-database solutions are visionaries and leaders. Yes, there are a select few open source companies that have started to work with the analytic vendors in the last couple of years. As expected, adoption is few and far between and lacks the depth and breadth, methodology, and proven successes. The leaders in the database market have developed mature, high-performance technologies to enable the heavy lifting of data for analysis. Because in-database processing can impact the performance of the database, it may require additional hardware purchases to handle the additional capacity for executing of analytics. As you consider in-database technology, vendors may ask for the following details to configure the right solution:

- *What is the largest size data to be processed in-database?* Whether it is small (in the gigabytes) or large (in the terabytes), in-database processing can impact the performance of your production data warehouse environment. Most of our customers who leverage in-database processing have a development or testing environment in a form of a data lab or sandbox to test before moving it into production.
- *Do you know the number of rows and columns of the data being analyzed in-database?* As mentioned, in-database processing can assist in joining, merging, and aggregating data in-database. It will help the consultants to estimate the amount of effort by knowing the rows and columns and type of data that will be processed in-database.

- *How many total users will have access to the in-database capabilities?* If your organization is laser focused on a department such as the operations research group to only have in-database technology, then the licensing and purchasing of the in-database solution can be minimal. On the other hand, if it is intended for enterprisewide usage, then expect a bigger investment in both software and hardware to accommodate the needs of the number of users for your business.
- *How many concurrent in-database sessions may be running?* In-database processing may be used in many concurrent sessions from an enterprise or departmental level to prepare the data and/or run the analytics. Depending on the size of your organization, consider one or two departments first to have access to in-database capabilities to show its value before enabling it enterprisewide.

In-database processing will require some retraining on how users handle, manage, and analyze the data. As you select the analytic or database vendor, consider how the users will need to transform the way they do things. For example, select a package that will minimally disrupt the current data preparation and analytic process. In another example, many analytic professionals will need to reuse existing code. If they are able to leverage the existing code and make minor tweaks, it will minimize the learning curve and disruption of culture within the company. It will likely gain acceptance and adoption when change is minimal.

I have demonstrated the value of in-database technology in an e-commerce company, telecommunication provider, and financial institution. In addition, I highlighted the importance of data quality and the in-database approach to accurately deliver data-driven decisions. Depending on your organization's needs for in-database, the investment can be minimal. Selecting the appropriate in-database solution from the right analytic and database vendor will make a big difference in value, adoption, and success. Now, let's move to in-memory analytics and reveal even more business benefits and value added from this technology.

ENDNOTES

1. Ekaterina Walter, "40 Eye-Opening Customer Service Quotes," *Forbes* (March 4, 2014), http://www.forbes.com/sites/ekaterinawalter/2014/03/04/40-eye-opening-customer-service-quotes/#14b64bc24dc8.
2. Wayne W. Eckerson, *Data Quality and the Bottom Line: Achieving Business Success through a Commitment to High Quality Data* (Chatsworth, CA: The Data Warehousing Institute, 2002). ©2002 by 101communications LLC.
3. Ibid.
4. Ibid.

CHAPTER 3

In-Memory Analytics

Data are a strategic asset, and organizations are collecting more data than ever before. The availability of so much data creates big opportunities but also bigger challenges on how to analyze *all* the data in a timely manner. Trends in analytics and data management, along with heightened regulatory and governance requirements, demand new, innovative approaches that can quickly transform massive volumes of data into meaningful and actionable insights. In-memory analytics help to overcome these challenges and enable organizations to analyze extremely large volumes of data very quickly and efficiently. This latest technological innovation provides an entirely new approach to tackle big data by using an in-memory analytics engine to deliver super-fast responses to complex analytical problems. Similar to in-database analytics, this technology eliminates the need to copy and replicate data and offers more superior benefits such as near real-time analyses.

BACKGROUND

Traditionally, computers have two types of data storage mechanisms—physical disk (hard drive) and RAM (random access memory). I can recall owning a computer with a floppy disk, 128MB of disk space and 4 MB of RAM; however those days are long gone. Now, I have the luxury of owning a laptop with a CD ROM drive, 500GB disk storage, and 8GB of RAM. The megabyte has transformed to gigabyte and beyond. In today's world, computers have much more available disk storage than RAM, but reading data from the disk is significantly slower—possibly hundreds of times—when compared to accessing the same data from RAM. Performance can be massively impacted when analyzing enormous volumes of data with the traditional disk-based technology.

In-memory analytics is an innovative approach to querying data when it resides in a computer's random access memory (RAM), as opposed to querying data stored on physical disks. This results in vastly shortened query response times, allowing business analytic applications to execute complex, data-intensive analytics and enable proactive data-driven decisions.

As the cost of RAM declines, in-memory analytics is becoming more feasible and affordable for many businesses. Analytic applications have traditionally supported caching data in RAM. Older 32-bit operating systems provided only 4 GB of addressable memory for analyses. But with the newer 64-bit operating systems, with up to 1 terabyte (TB) of addressable memory (and could be more in the future), technology has made it feasible to cache larger volumes of data—potentially an entire data warehouse or data mart—in a computer's RAM.

In addition to providing incredibly fast query response times, in-memory analytics can reduce and eliminate the need for data indexing and storing pre-aggregated data or aggregating your data to conserve time. This capability tremendously reduces IT costs and enables faster implementation of analytic applications. It is anticipated that as analytic applications embrace in-memory analytics, complex data models, data visualization, and analytics processes can be executed much faster with more accuracy and precision.

Customers are still exploring and learning about in-memory analytics since it is relatively new. This technology was introduced around 2011. Customers who have adopted in-memory analytics are experiencing near real-time analyses with deeper insights and increased performance. It allows them to do more with the data they have and to solve a variety of business problems that were previously not possible. As complex data exploration and analytical approaches (descriptive analytics, predictive analytics, machine learning, text analytics, prescriptive analytics, etc.) become more prevalent, the efficiencies of integrating both the data and analytical workloads are critical to handling the processing needs in today's business climate of unpredictability and change.

TRADITIONAL APPROACH

As a consumer of IT, I am used to storing my data on a hard drive on my PC or a local server and access it when it is needed. When applying analytics, it is no different. The process is similar but it might not be so simple having all the data being readily available. Conventionally, the data are stored on a disk in a server room, and business analysts are given permission to access the data for analysis.

In the traditional batch processing of data, IT personnel have to deal with managing a lot of data back and forth between disks and data shuffling to obtain the right data. This process can create a lot of headaches and complexity for IT and business.

Our customers have encountered these common challenges, regardless of the industry or the size of the organization:

1. *Network impact*: There is a large impact on I/O (input/output) time and resources when dealing with large volumes of data for analytics. To minimize this impact, an organization needs optimized file structure and high-speed database access methods. Thus, in-memory analytics overcomes this process by moving all the data and workload into memory for analysis.
2. *Data aggregation*: Aggregating data can take a lot of processing time. It is common practice to store aggregated data in an independent data mart for users to access and run queries when needed. In addition, coding is needed to optimize the aggregation algorithm to improve performance, and it is a time consuming task. Thus, with in-memory technology, data aggregation process is not required, and this can save both time and money for any organization.
3. *Data movement*: Moving the data is risky and hazardous. When data are moved, copies are stored on a separate server, which creates redundant data and a silo data store that will need to be managed.

Some of the approaches taken to overcome the limitations of physical disk storage include having hardware/software to micromanage where the data are actually stored on the physical platter. The more frequent the data are accessed, the closer to the spindle the data are stored, whereas less frequently accessed data could be written to the outside of the platters.

Now let's examine in-memory analytics in detail and discuss how it works.

IN-MEMORY ANALYTICS APPROACH

Compared to the traditional method of executing complex and advanced analytics, in-memory analytics offers many advantages and is an innovative approach to analyzing large amounts of data. In-memory analytics is a technique in which all the data used by an analytic application are stored within the main memory of the computing environment. In most cases, the computing environment is a data warehouse. Instead of accessing the data from a physical disk, data remain in the data warehouse until needed. Data are then lifted into RAM memory for analytics. Since the data are kept in memory, multiple users can share data across various applications and the time of any calculation is extremely fast, in a secure and parallel environment. In-memory analytics also takes advantage of multithreading and distributed computing, where you can distribute the data (and complex workloads that process the data) across multiple nodes in clusters as shown in Figure 3.1.

Figure 3.1 In-memory analytics

There are significant differences between traditional and in-memory processing. The first and most significant difference between the traditional and in-memory approach is *where the data are stored* for analytics. Today, with the powerful hardware available commercially, customers are taking advantage of in-memory processing power instead of constantly transferring, meddling, or shuffling with data residing on the disk. In the case of in-memory analytics, the persistent storage of the data is still on the physical disk, but the data are read into memory when needed for analytics. The second difference and biggest advantage compared to traditional processing is *speed*. In-memory processing allows users to keep the data in memory and run iterative processing or jobs without having to go back and forth to the disk each time. The end users can quickly get answers without worrying about the infrastructure limitations for analytical experiments or testing. In addition, data scientists are not restricted to a sample of data. They have all of the data and can apply as many analytic techniques and iterations as desired to find the best model in near real-time.

As indicated in Chapter 1, the Analytical Data Life Cycle, in-memory analytics is not only associated with queries and data exploration/visualization, but is also used with more complex processes like predictive analytics, complex model development, and text analytics. For example, regression, correlations, decision trees, and neural networks are all associated with in-memory analytics processing.

In-memory analytics helps to solve the following issues that the traditional approach is unable to resolve:

- *Obtaining immediate analytical insights from multiple data sources*: In-memory processing can support complex analytical workloads with parallel scaling for increased performance as compared to the traditional architecture. What has previously taken days or weeks to analyze via complex analytical models for strategic insights can now be executed in seconds and minutes. We will illustrate this with examples later in this chapter.
- *Analyzing granular and deeper analytical insights using the entire data set as opposed to working with a small subset*: You can now take

advantage of this innovative technology to uncover meaningful new opportunities, mitigate unknown risks, and drive growth for your business with near real-time insights. An example of the benefit of this is with clustering/segmenting data. Typically, when clustering data, you end up with several large clusters, as well as some small ones. It's these smaller clusters that typically contain the "interesting" group (as the larger clusters are the "typical or average" groups. If we had to subset due to limitations with estimating the model, there is a very strong chance that we would have missed the interesting observations (as we don't know what constitutes interesting—that's the point of the clustering).

- *Integrating digital data with new demographics and external audience*: This is the ability to be preemptive in analyzing tweets, postings, and texts. In order to gain competitive advantage, organizations need to discover, analyze, and proactively respond to different, changing, and fast-moving events that occur in volume (e.g., in 2015 there were, on average, 6,000 tweets per second). These events of interest are only apparent when they are understood and heard by the dependent parts of the organization. This requires event processing that follows through the organization in contextually and relevant data-driven actions. The ability to ingest data and process streams of events effectively identifies patterns and correlations of importance, focusing organizational activity to react and even proactively drive the results they seek and respond to in real time. It has become a directive for many companies to not just maintain but continue to push the envelope to be faster and better with in-memory analytics.

Similar to in-database analytics, a data warehouse is an essential component of in-memory analytics, especially since it contains a set of data that is integrated, cleansed, and refined. Data exploration and visualization is ideal for in-memory processing because it can quickly visualize and provide useful information, such as correlation on the data that you are working with, in order to determine whether and what type of further analysis is needed. One customer expressed the value that it can "show me the data and patterns in the data." In addition, in-memory analytics allows for more self-service for end users because there will be less dependence on IT to create, maintain, and administer aggregates and indexes of the data. In-memory analytics also helps meet diverse and unplanned workloads (e.g., discover relationships or build models involving observations at granular level).

THE NEED FOR IN-MEMORY ANALYTICS

In-memory analytics is becoming the new or next generation BI (business intelligence). Many of the vendors in this space have developed visually rich analytics features with click, drag-and-drop capabilities. With easy access to data and analytics, organizations are adopting in-memory analytics to develop interactive dashboards and explore data without limits. There are a few vendors that offer in-memory for predictive analytics and data model development. With in-memory technology, business users can now engage their data with blazing speed, resulting in more informed, proactive, data-driven decisions. For IT departments, in-memory analytics offers far less time spent on data analysis, aggregate data, performance tuning, and other time-consuming tasks.

Gartner Research confirms that not only can data be retrieved faster, but in-memory analytical technology performs complex calculations and query results much significantly faster than disk-based approaches. This allows users to dissect data and create robust reporting without the limitations associated with traditional Business Intelligence (BI) tools such as multidimensional cubes or aggregate tables. Near real-time, ad-hoc query capabilities can be extended to even high volume and velocity transaction–based industries such as financial services, telecommunication, and retail.

Organizations are adopting in-memory analytics to solve many issues in conjunction with the traditional approach and seeing the need to improve performance, economics, and governance. The needs are very similar to in-database analytics and become the main drivers for many organizations. What follows are some reasons for in-memory analytics.

Complex analytics requirements

Traditional IT infrastructures present a number of challenges, and one of them is to overcome the slow query performance supporting complex analytical requirements. It simply cannot keep pace with today's changing and dynamic data management and analytical requirements for fast and accurate analysis. In addition, it is not designed to process complex analytics on terabytes (or beyond) of data efficiently. This is where in-memory analytics can help. In-memory analytics can solve complex analytics that is often coupled with large data volumes.

Growing big data volumes

Many enterprises are being perplexed by a massive explosion of data in their databases and analytics applications. Exponential growth of data is being captured and stored, along with semi-structured forms of data files such as email, video, and freeform text (such as tweets, Facebook comments/status, yelp comments, and other social media sources). At the same time tighter regulations put the burden on companies to maintain and store data available for years to come in case of audits or requests from law enforcement agencies. In-memory analysis makes access and analysis of large data volumes possible at incredibly fast speed and yields a higher return on investment.

Less reliance on IT

With the presence of big data and the explosion of data-driven applications, organizations are discovering it is becoming harder to manage their data and analytical projects for all levels of the organization. With the traditional approaches, the queries and reporting are taking too long to execute because it takes too long to manipulate the data. In-memory analytics eliminates complicated disk-based shuffling of data. There will be no need to wait for the IT bottleneck to build summary and aggregated tables to be used for analysis from the disk-based data. Business units can be more self-serving with in-memory analytics. One customer has expressed the opinion that it has driven a wider adoption of analytics because of the speed it offers to the users throughout the enterprise.

Enhanced user interface

Vendors have developed very attractive and intuitive interactive data visualization solutions, which have been adopted as the common front-end interface to analytical applications. With their intuitive displays, it is new paradigm for business analysts and IT users who aren't accustomed to the grid style of analysis and reporting offered by relational databases and spreadsheets. Interacting and exploring data using in-memory visualization tools offer very user friendly tasks such as clicking on a pie chart or dragging data onto a scatter plot—and the ability to easily visualize the relationship of their data is a trendy concept.

Departmental application

In-memory analytics is ideal for departmental applications, as users can analyze the full depth and breadth of their data since there are no practical limits to performing drill-down style capabilities. Customers who have adopted in-memory analytics are able to facilitate a more exploratory, visual analysis of big data with easy-to-use data selection and access to common graphical user interface components such as sliders, radio boxes, and check boxes offered via the user interface. I interact with customers who have in-memory analytics for enterprise use as well as customers who have used it for common departmental deployments, but it is more commonly for departmental deployment.

Although the need for in-memory analytics is still growing, I am seeing huge benefits from customers who have either adopted the technology or implemented in-memory analytics within their organization. Let's examine these business and IT benefits.

Benefits

Depending on the size of the organization and the use of in-memory analytics, the benefits are truly remarkable. Customers who implemented in-memory analytics see big transformations of their processes, productivity, and culture within IT and business. There is a good balance of the tangible and intangible benefits using in-memory analytics.

Dramatic performance improvements

Users are querying and interacting with data in-memory, which is significantly faster than accessing data from disk to execute complex analytics that are data volume intensive. In one case, a customer decreased processing in a regression model from 167 hours down to 84 seconds. More success stories are to come in the next section.

Discover new, interesting insights

In-memory analytics can give business users rapid execution of complex analytics to deliver new levels of interesting insights to optimize business performance or improve the decision making process without the IT bottleneck. Many of the customers tell me that it provides self-service applications to quickly explore and visualize data for discovery.

Cost effective

The in-memory approach provides the ability to analyze very large data sets at any time with any data type, and customers are expressing that it is much simpler to administer. As IT is not burdened with data movement and performance tuning of the ETL process, it minimizes the resources and increases cost savings.

Some of the intangible benefits that customers have stated the following.

Ease of use leads to higher adoption of use

The most valuable benefit that organizations are experiencing, albeit less recognized because it is an intangible one, is that the ease of use which leads to high adoption rate. In-memory analytic software allows business analysts and line-of-business managers to build their own reports, charts, graphs, and/or dashboards with very little training or technical expertise because of the intuitive interface that allows user to simply click, drag, and drop data for analysis. This also encourages significant higher levels of user adoption due to the autonomy and sense of ownership that business analysts and nontechnical personnel have to explore their own data and not feel intimidated with the data and technology. The ultimate benefit is the transformation shifts away from those that manage the data to the stakeholders who use, own, and analyze the data. In-memory analytics enable users to comprehend and expose their business in new ways and interactively explore big data without limits.

Offloading work from the overburdened data warehouse

In-memory analytics offers the wonderful benefit of eliminating a big chunk of repetitive and expensive (in terms of CPU usage and disk I/O) processing that would normally be time consuming and add to the burden placed on the database or data warehouse servers. With in-memory analytics, the analytics engine pulls the data into memory from the data warehouse or database once or when it is needed. This process can be scheduled to populate the data as a batch or incremental load and/or overnight during off-peak hours. Thus, it alleviates the capacity demand by offloading the query from the data warehouse or database during peak interactive hours of the day. By unburdening the database server or data warehouse, organizations can benefit from delivering faster performance, producing more reports per hour, and free up capacity on the source database servers or data warehouse for other data queries and purposes.

Enabling self-service applications for departments

Companies are realizing the value of convenience and availability by setting up a mechanism for departments or workgroup to leverage in-memory analytics. I see two camps, one for the power users and the other for specific departments such as sales or marketing. In one extreme case, customers are setting up environments for power users to conduct high-performance analytics using in-memory technology and limiting its use to perhaps the PhDs or statisticians. On the other hand, organizations are realizing the benefit of self-service environments for larger user groups for sales and marketing to operate autonomously using in-memory technology without impacting the data warehouse workload.

Ad-hoc analysis

Ad-hoc analysis is very limited or nonexistent in the traditional approach because it can take a significant amount of time to obtain the data from disk. In-memory analytics makes it possible to conduct ad-hoc analysis because of its infrastructure—data are only lifted into memory when they are needed for analysis. And it is in the true sense of the word, ad-hoc. In-memory analytics provides the ability to rapidly lift the data from the database or data warehouse and users can explore, discover, and build an analytic application to meet a specific task at hand. For example, let's consider exploring the relationship of age groups and recent usage of coupons that are delivered to customers via emails or smart phones. In this case, the analysis is undertaken and then programs can be built to offer more coupons and bigger incentives to the most loyal customers with even deeper discounts. It could be a flash sale or limited offers to attract customers and increase sales.

Now that the benefits are explained, let's examine the justification for in-memory analytics.

Getting Started

As mentioned earlier, in-memory is relatively new; it is has been on the market for approximately four years (at time of writing). As with all new technology, there are questions about its capabilities and the value it brings into an organization. Customers often have an analytics strategy and roadmap in mind before discussing the in-memory analytics approach. Here are some things that you should consider to justify and get you started with in-memory analytics.

Identify a business problem or opportunity and consider what users do with the data

Start by identifying the problem or opportunity. This is often perceived as a "no brainer," but it can be the most time-consuming and resource-intensive process. Every business has issues or problems but identifying "just" one to perform a proof of value or proof of concept can be daunting. Customers definitely want to get the "biggest bang for the buck" effort, but not every problem can or should be solved with in-memory technology. However, if your organization is report-oriented and the infrastructure does not facilitate what-if analysis, interactive exploration of data, discovery of data patterns, and new opportunities, then adopting an in-memory technology can definitely be beneficial. I always suggest to start small and grow/expand as needed once you are able to solve one problem, and people will see value with the new technology.

Understand the IT and business bottlenecks

With any organization, there are bottlenecks to any process. Are the users expressing grievances about poor query response times? Do complex queries and analytical computations time out before completing? Does poor performance prevent users and executives from asking important business questions or any questions? If so, consider in-memory technology that delivers an integrated data management and analytics for the ultimate user experience. It is critical that the technology does not constrain users but offers flexibility and scalability in terms of data access, analysis, and reporting.

Assess the costs and balance with the expected benefits

In-memory analytics will require some investment from the company in terms of new hardware, new software, professional services, and definitely training. Since an in-memory deployment involves supporting another data structure and analysis, it will need to involve support from IT and business sides to work together. In-memory investments have delivered great value and benefits from the customers that I work with, but the benefits and value added may be hard to quantify and articulate to the leadership team. On one hand, the business side often is not aware of tangible, lower cost of ownership benefits such as saving disk space, minimizing data movement, integrating the platform, and reducing administrative labor that would otherwise be required to make these queries run faster and more efficient. On the other hand, you may have the IT side that would have to support the hardware maintenance and may not see the intangible benefits of ease of use, access for business analysts, and ad-hoc capabilities, so bringing the two sides together is critical. Organizations contemplating in-memory analytics often would develop a business case to justify the investment. Positioning in-memory analytics with the user communities and types of applications is critical in the cost/benefit analysis and overall analytics strategy.

Obtain a corporate, senior executive sponsor

All of the prospects and customers that I work with say that having a senior corporate sponsor for in-memory projects is a must. Many projects fail to go forward (even after spectacular results) due to having no senior management sponsorship. The sponsor provides not only the financial support but also guidance on how to maneuver the political push-backs within IT and business sides. In addition, this sponsor can help to identify the business problem that will help to drive innovation and increase the bottom line. Without a sponsor, it is very challenging to justify the investment of new hardware, software, services, and training.

Finally, it is vital that you involve all parties—IT, business users, and sponsors—early in the decision process, as well as throughout the practical side. When they participate in the decision process, I witness higher success rate and on-time, on-budget delivery of tasks.

Requirements

Many vendors in the in-memory analytics space offer similar technologies, features, functionality, and infrastructure. However, the success or failure of in-memory analytics does rest to some degree on the technology selected to be the delivery platform. Customers who adopted this technology say that the platform needs to be web-enabled/centric as their primary requirement. Beyond the web-enabled requirement, here are some other essential technology-driven prerequisites to consider.

Integration with your existing integrated data warehouse and business intelligence

The need for a data warehouse is still prevalent for in-memory analytics. While some vendors convey or advertise that in-memory analytics does not require or avoid developing a data warehouse, this option may work for smaller organizations that have only a single data source or a small system. However, for larger companies that typically have multiple data sources or larger, more complex systems, the data warehouse is still the ideal platform to capture, transform, and integrate the data for analysis. This is where the in-database capability can be part of the overall infrastructure. As you explore and look for in-memory technology, make sure that it can be integrated with the existing data warehouse and BI environments. An in-memory solution normally comes with visualization capabilities, and it can tap into the BI applications and data warehouse to uncover data patterns, build complex data models, and deliver to the web or mobile devices for enterprise consumption.

Enterprise scalability

Most if not all customers tend to start small with an appliance to enable in-memory analytics for a specific department. Once proven to show value and a positive ROI, the vast majority (9 out of 10) customers upgrade to a bigger appliance and add more memory (via the addition of nodes) to handle additional data for high-performance analyses. Therefore, it is important to select a solution that can scale linearly as you grow. When you add more data, more complex analytics, more analytical data models, and more data, ensure that the technology can scale to support today's and tomorrow's requirements. Therefore, it is critical that you select a solution that can provide enterprise-class infrastructure that enables you to be strategic and expand.

Ensure near real-time data refresh

Whether you create reports or build an analytical data model, data are extracted from a source system, most likely from a data warehouse. In-memory analytics load the data directly from the source system into in-memory nodes, and data latency can be a concern. There are SLAs (service-level agreements) where reports or analytics have to be delivered within a specific window of time. Therefore, an in-memory solution will need high-speed connectivity to the data source or data warehouse so that the data can be extracted ad-hoc or otherwise can be scheduled for incremental data loads during off-peak hours. Having the flexibility to refresh data in near real-time for in-memory analytics is a powerful benefit for data-driven decisions.

Data governance and security

Depending on the vendor you select and the infrastructure for in-memory analytics, there is a higher potential risk of expositing data to more end users than ever. This raises data security concerns:

- How the data are accessed
- Who has access to the data
- Where it is stored
- How much data is analyzed
- Who can see and share the data and analyses
- Whether it can be pushed to mobile devices for information sharing

In recent months, we witnessed data security breaches globally in both the private and public sectors. Thus, selecting a solution that focuses on heightening data governance and making data security a priority can alleviate major headaches, costly remedies, and public embarrassment. I highly recommend a vendor that had a solution around a centralized data server such as a data warehouse or database. Having a centralized data repository option enables IT to govern the data in a highly safeguarded environment. With a centralized data repository, such as a data warehouse, your in-memory analytics can adapt and conform to your organization's data security measures. Another recommendation is to identify the users with certain rights and privileges to access sensitive data, analyze, and store the data and adjust as the employees change their role or job function within the company.

Let's examine some customer successes and case studies. These customers have adopted, implemented, and achieved superior results using in-memory analytics by considering the above requirements.

SUCCESS STORIES AND USE CASES

There are a number of success stories and use cases for in-memory analytics since its inception into the industry. As previously mentioned, in-memory analytics is used to explore the data and model development. While in-database analytics started to catch on in the mid- to late-2000s, in-memory analytics was first commercially promoted in 2011 with SAS and Teradata.

Global Financial Company: Explore and Analyze Sales and Business Operations

Our first success story comes from a global banking and financial services company based in Europe. This institution has an international network spanning 50 markets with more than 9,000 branches and over 149,000 employees. This commercial bank operates in 22 European countries, and its strategic position in Western and Eastern Europe gives the company one of the region's highest market shares.

One of the reasons for it adopting and implementing in-memory analytics is to enhance its data governance focus. It was and still is imperative for a financial company to adhere to rules and regulations, especially when it comes to data security and governance. Protecting customer information is a priority for the company.

There are three main objectives mandated by the CFO (chief financial officer) to improve and implement change for the future of the company:

1. The first one is to streamline and optimize their internal processes. Their traditional process took too long to get the information to sales and executives to make data-driven decisions. The data latency had become an issue and was impacting their competitiveness and hence growth.
2. The second is to create strategic value and develop a long-term strategy that can transform the company from reactive to proactive with updated technologies and near real-time information to be used across the enterprise.
3. Finally, the third is to create a diverse marketing campaign with various promotions and incentives for customers, to grow their customer base and profitability. In Figure 3.2, the customer illustrates the initiatives for the adoption of in-memory analytics.

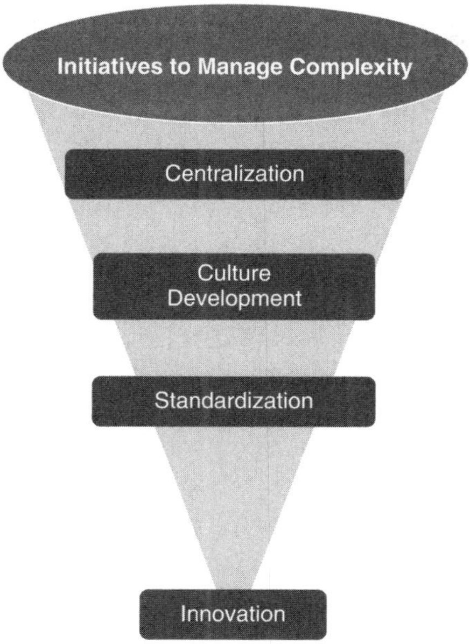

Figure 3.2 CFO mandate for the project

The CFO is the executive sponsor for this project, and he has outlined the key areas and initiatives to manage complexity and simplify the need for information sharing across departments and throughout the enterprise.

Centralization

This is the first and most critical initiative for the customer. Over the years, data has grown exponentially and been stored in many locations that users can access. The many silos of data created issues in areas of data management, data capture, data tagging, and data quality. Since there was no central repository of data such as an integrated data warehouse, there were many data silos that created inconsistent data analyses and reporting to management and staff. Centralizing all data into a data warehouse defines a consistent process to capture, integrate, and access the data for analytics and analyses. In addition, centralizing the data will provide you a single repository for analysis and enhance the data governance focus to adhere to policies and regulations.

Culture development

This is an intangible initiative that encourages IT and business to work together. It is expected and understood that IT manages the data warehouse and supports the needs of the business side. Thus, it is critical and an imperative to adopt an integrated solution that closely connects analytics and data management to be supported by IT and business. In addition, the integrated solution would be shared across departments and business units that include executives, managers, commercial units, and product lines. The culture development initiative is to create an open organization of information sharing but also focus on synergies across all departments to be more collaborative.

Standardization

There has not been a standard tool or process to address advanced analytics. The bank has been using various technologies including in-house development and commercial products. In addition, business reports are not consistent in quality and consistency for management to make decisions. By standardizing on one analytics solution and on one platform, the goal is to streamline the process, reduce the amount of *number crunching*, and increase the efforts behind *study and analysis*. It is a way to leverage resources to be less operational and to become more strategic in their roles and responsibilities. By doing so, information can be distributed in a timely manner and across the enterprise with one consistent view of the business.

Innovation

By combining the efforts behind centralization, culture development, and standardization, the bank's CFO ultimately wants to drive and deliver innovation to increase profitability and the bottom line. This company believes innovation can be achieved with the adoption of advanced analytics to analyze customer behavior, customer relationships, predictive simulations, and profitability of the business. It is also a strategy to move the business into the twenty-first century to support strategic decision making and sustain the competitiveness of the business.

The traditional approach to analyzing sales and business operations is at best mediocre. Data reside in many silos and there are many copies of the same data. Thus, the analyses of the data can be misleading and results are not trustworthy, as data may be outdated and there is not a process to provide a single view of the customer. Analyzing customer data and reporting the results from the analyses are critical for the business. The traditional model does not allow business analysts to analyze large amounts of data at a granular level. The staff spent as much as 85% of their time preparing the data instead of performing the analysis.

The business is asking for an innovative solution that allows analysis with a growing level of granularity, on large amounts of data, down to each single deal transaction and enables the staff to be more focused on data analysis instead of data preparation. Thus, in-memory analytics enters the picture to help the business thrive with a single, fast, scalable, and user-friendly solution.

Transformation Focus

As the bank examines its business, it considers many options and concludes that they need an advanced analytics solution focusing on data governance. Figure 3.3 illustrates the before and after picture of the architecture.

Figure 3.3 illustrates how the traditional architecture is set up and used by the bank. The silo model has data sources (legacy systems, payment systems, securities, markets products, and customer info) in various data silos. As the data enters into the system, each group such as controller, risk, accounting, and regulations applies different data management process and services. Because there is no consistent method to manage the data, it is a "spaghetti" mess of data warehouse coming and going everywhere. Since the data may be in an inconsistent format or not integrated with other data sources, the company has a challenge to trust the state of the data and the results of the analyses from the data. In addition, with four silo data marts potentially storing duplicate data, it requires more resources to manage and maintain. This is what

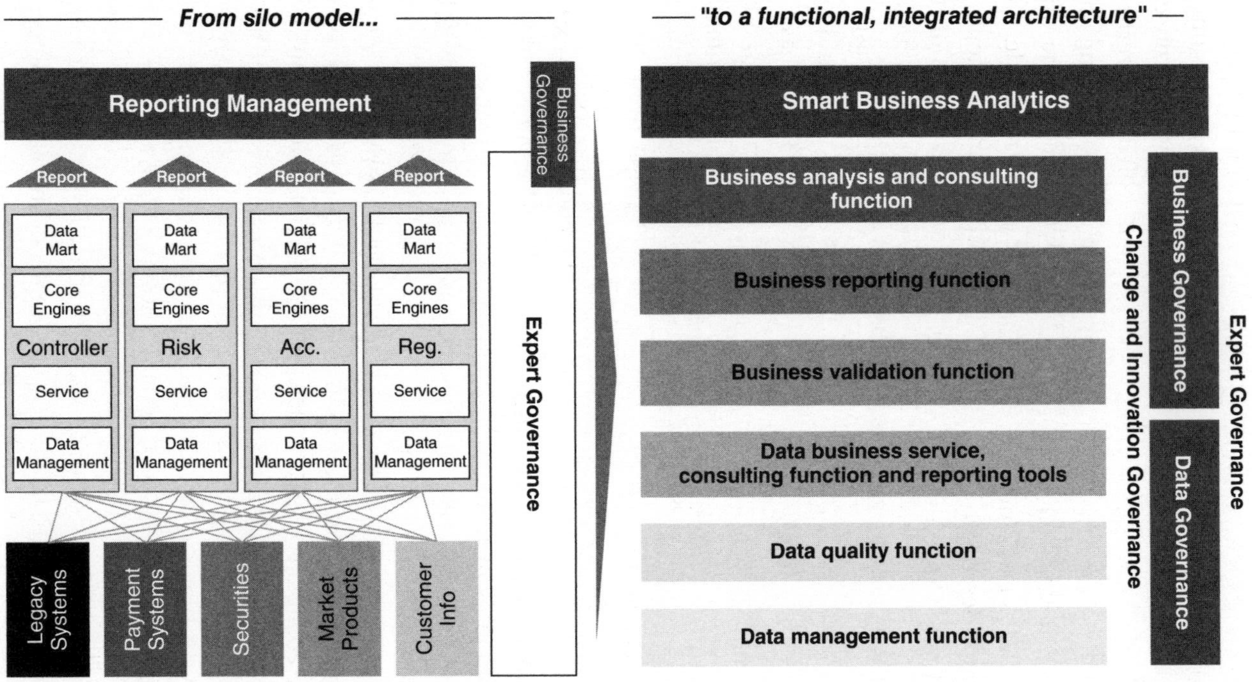

Figure 3.3 From silos model to a functional, integrated architecture

the bank referred to as "number crunching" from the previous section. Ultimately, different reports are being delivered and management is unable to trust which report is correct to make business decisions.

Transforming the left side to the right side, the layering concept is much more streamlined and with a lot of emphasis on data governance. Analytics have become the focal point instead of just reporting on the data. The company truly believes in using analytics to drive data-driven decisions. Let's examine the new architecture on the right side.

When I described the centralization, culture development, and standardization initiatives, the new architecture provides all of these elements. As data enter into the architecture, there is a standard process of managing and integrating the data. One important aspect to highlight is the focus on data quality, which is a topic that I find many customers tend to ignore and not address. (Refer to in-database data quality from Chapter 2.) In this case, the customer carves out a layer to address data quality issues so that data is cleansed and integrated before it gets analyzed. Each business unit such as controlling, risk, accounting, and regulation leverages the same data from one centralized repository to analyze and run reports using one view of the data. There are cross-functional layers for IT and business to govern the data. Figure 3.4 provides a more granular view of the architecture and how data is governed from IT and business.

The bank no longer has four data marts but one enterprise data warehouse (EDW) to allow IT to stage and store the data. Once the data are captured in the EDW, data mining and reporting tools are available to analyze the data for the various business units. The advanced analytics are applied to the EDW data, where the business can further do analysis such as validating and reporting. In the next section, we will examine how in-memory analytics is used at this financial institution.

In-Memory Analytics for Visualization and Reporting

The CFO has three main goals for this project:

- Ensure a coherent and synergistic implementation process of systems for use from executives to line of business managers to sales.

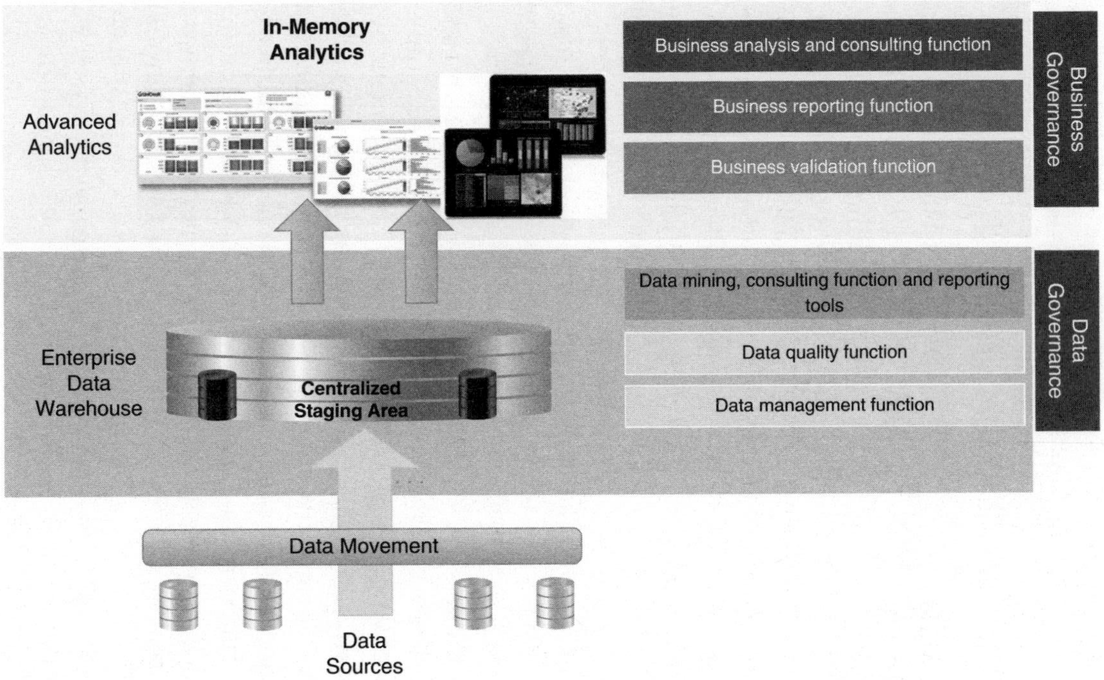

Figure 3.4 Integrating data and analytics

- Provide all management levels and commercial personnel reports and network analysis in near real-time.
- Standardize the rules and methodologies used at all levels to measure the phenomenon of risk-adjusted performance.

In-memory analytics was adopted by the customer and is used extensively for data visualization and exploration to create reports for executives and publish the results to the portal. One area is sales. In the banking world, there are many offers and incentives for credit cards, loans, and other types of accounts. For example, everyone can relate to applying for a loan and wondering if you can qualify (and how much you can borrow) to purchase a car, house, or renovation project. The bank uses in-memory analytics to analyze customer data at a granular level to examine historical data: whether you have applied for a loan before and were either accepted or rejected; you have employment and steady income to pay back the loan; whether you have defaulted on a loan in the past; and use of your credit history and credit score to see how much you can qualify for. These are some basic and rudimentary data exploration techniques used by the bank that require it to be near real-time so that it can provide an immediate response to the applicant. Figure 3.5 illustrates the process.

Once the data reside in the data warehouse, the process begins with data preparation to ensure the data are in the required format. The data are then lifted into memory for analysis. Analytics explores the relationship of the data and runs simulations to provide the output and scenarios based on the input of the applicant in seconds. It then provides the mechanism to create a report that can be published to the portal, a dashboard, or email, or even mobile devices.

In addition to sales, this institution uses in-memory analytics to analyze its network operations. It analyzes network capacity and the behavior of the network to adequately support the business planning. It does not want to have any downtime for any of their systems, as it can drastically affect the business operations and loss of revenue.

What used to take days and hours to process and analyze is now taking minutes and seconds. From analyzing loan applications to monitoring the network operations for business planning, the bank has expanded its use of in-memory analytics from 1,300 users in

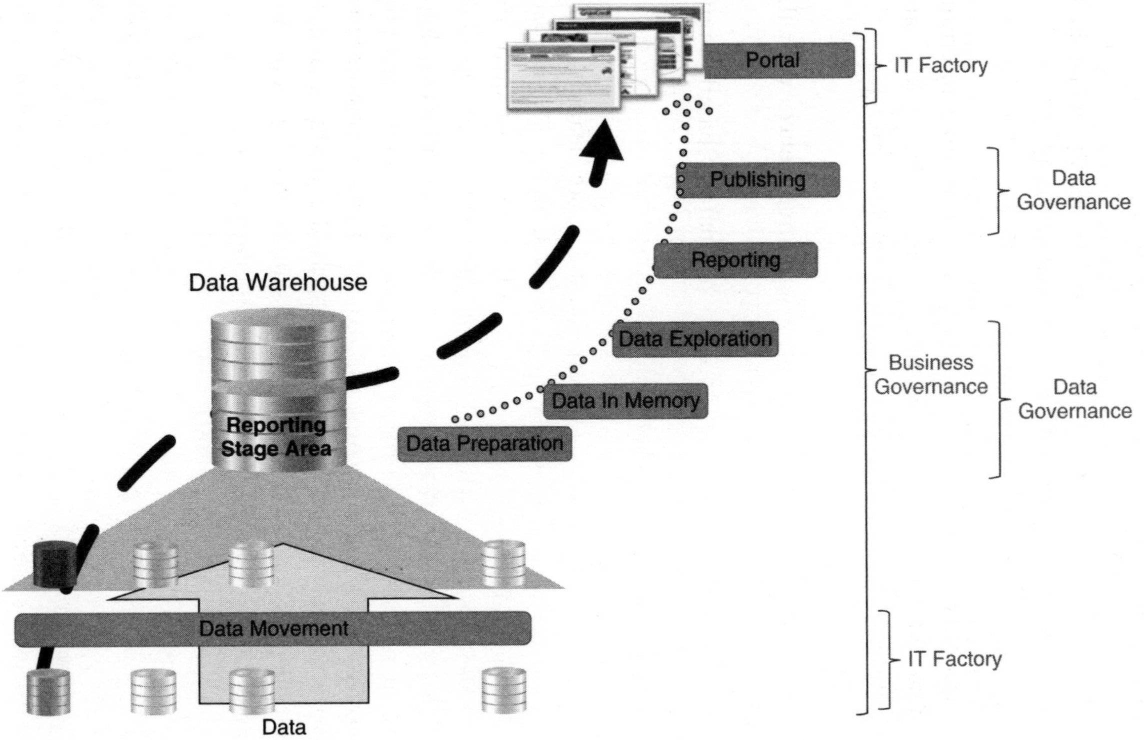

Figure 3.5 In-memory analytics process

2013 to over 15,000 users today. The user-friendly interface and game-changing performance have made this transformation a success. In-memory analytics offer the following benefits:

- Specialization of supported processed with definition of a single point of access for corporate center and network
- Optimization of workflow information
- Centralization of information construction in order to ensure data ad information consistency across CFO, CRO, and network, creating the conditions for recurring synergies
- Centralization of data quality
- Centralization of expertise of business intelligence, with the creation of a service facilities server hub
- More productive from analysts with less data preparation time

Best Practices and Lessons Learned

The customer shared some best practices and lesson learned when adopting a new technology such as in-memory analytics. The primary takeaway from this bank is that the business side must drive the project, while leveraging on IT for support. The business side included the IT side very early on when it evaluated the tools and technology. Because in-memory analytics was relatively new and emerging, the customer started several discussions with various vendors that included a proof-of-concept that aligns with the business and IT initiatives (centralization, standardization, culture development, and innovation). Other best practices and lessons learned are:

- *Obtain executive sponsorship*: A strong sponsorship from an executive is imperative. In this case, it is the CFO who oversees the project, manages change with the business and IT sides, and reviews processes from the traditional to the new architecture. Having a strong executive sponsorship is fundamental to the success of this project.
- *Develop a glossary*: Since business and IT must intertwine, the bank developed a glossary of definitions to define terms,

process, and taxonomy. We often have a different understanding of a term. This glossary standardizes terms that are used by both IT and business. As each process gets developed, the glossary is updated and shared across the enterprise.

- *Involve all parties early in the process*: The CFO brought in the business side to drive the requirements of the project and leverage IT to support the infrastructure. Both the IT and business staff help to define the data preparation process, since it is the first step to getting the data into the EDW. Both teams were involved to certify the data so that it is correctly governed to protect the integrity of the business. In addition, by getting all the groups involved early, there is more likelihood for success once the technology was selected as each group has input into the selection of the solution.
- *Select an integrated solution*: This is a critical best practice consideration that is to have analytics well integrated with the enterprise data warehouse. In addition, the integrated solution must deliver end-to-end capabilities from data preparation, data exploration, advanced analytics, and reporting. Finally, the integrated solution should include hardware and software with a strong architecture to scale linearly as needed for today's needs and the future.

These best practices and lessons learned provide a good perspective of the efforts of teamwork and investment needed to be successful. The bank continues to expand the use of in-memory analytics. Because the adoption rate has been so high, in-memory analytics will extend to beyond 15,000 users and to more departments. It will continue to publish information and reports to mobile devices for data-driven decisions.

European Government Agency: Analyze Tax and Population Data

Thus far, I have provided a few customer successes in the financial, e-commerce, and telecommunications sector. This next one highlights the use of in-memory analytics in the public sector. It is a government agency based in Europe that handles taxes for individual, business, and customs for the entire country. As the population changes, this agency is also in charge of analyzing census data, which is very high in volume. The agency is collecting more data today than ever to manage the changing needs of the population.

In the traditional architecture, many of the business units such as customs, tax, financial, enforcement, and social services benefits did not have an automated way to look at the data. They relied on manual lookups and paper trail to know whether an individual household paid their property tax, as illustrated in Figure 3.6. This is just one example of their archaic process.

Similar to the financial institution discussed earlier, this agency has data in many silos. There is no standardized process to manage the massive amounts of collected data.

Once the data are collected, applying analytics is a challenge and time consuming. The reason is the number of analytical tools and process to analyze the silos of data, and each department had its own types of tools to use. A standard tool is needed with the analytical capabilities to meet all of the departments' needs. When analytics is used, it can take hours and days to complete due to the infrastructure and the silos of data that need to be consolidated. It is currently inefficient for the IT and business groups to operate on a daily basis, motivating the agency to change to support the growth of the country and its population.

In-Memory Analytics

The homegrown, in-house application that is developed and being used is no longer able to meet the needs of the agency. When the

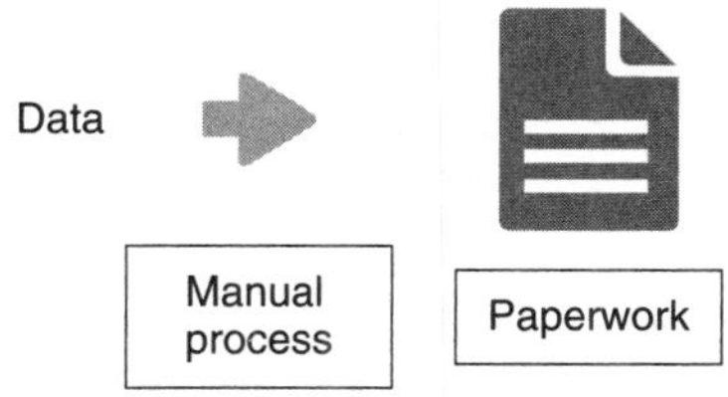

Figure 3.6 Manual lookup and paperwork

agency was exploring for a new analytics package, they considered many factors. First and foremost is the usability of the interface. It has to be easy to use, and anyone from an analyst to director level can use the technology without have to do any coding and offer self-service functionality. Another factor was the depth and breadth of the analytics capability from beginner to novice to data statisticians. The technology must be scalable and fast when analyzing large amounts of data from many sources. After many months of evaluating, this agency selected an in-memory data visualization package that can be integrated with their existing data warehouse.

In-memory data visualization is used in various business units because of its flexibility, depth and breadth, ease of use, and timely analysis. One great example from this agency is the ability to create a dashboard for tax collectors. Prior to this system, all records were manually managed and monitored with paper trails. With in-memory analytics, the data can be analyzed at the granular level that includes all of the customer information—name, address, property tax value, tax owed or paid, and so on. The tax collector can simply leverage the information from the dashboard on a mobile device and determine who has not paid their taxes, as shown in Figure 3.7. The tax collector can receive alerts from those who have not paid their taxes and are overdue for 30, 60, 90 days, and beyond. When the tax collector visits the household to collect the taxes, the debt can be showed to the clients in real time on the dash board and there can be no argument as to whether the client claims to have paid or not. It offers a dynamic application for the tax collector to update and manage the data. Once the information is updated from the mobile device, it updates the dashboard for everyone in the agency to view and see the progress.

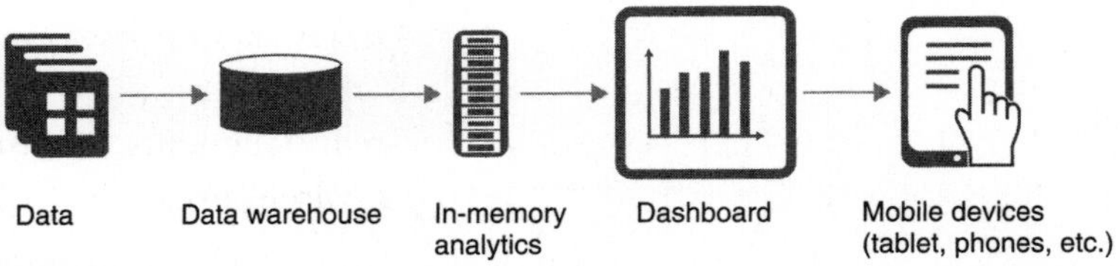

Figure 3.7 Distribution of information

This is a great example of using in-memory analytics to get real-time feeds and results and increase revenue for the agency.

In addition to the tax department, another use of in-memory analytics is from the customs department. As the agency gets many incoming packages to its country, it collects the data and filters what may be interesting for the inspectors to flag and inspect. With in-memory analytics, data are being fed as packages are being scanned, and the data is analyzed for any suspicious materials for further examination. This type of information is shared with the line of business and executives to ensure the safety of the country and its citizens. Other uses for in-memory analytics and data visualization from this agency include:

- Analyze and examine resources to support the needs of the agency for future growth.
- Determine if the agency has funding for the government to spend on special projects or upgrades to their facility.
- Segment customers in neighborhoods to better serve the community by providing additional police patrols or enforcement services.
- Analyze census population and determine the growth or decline in certain neighborhoods and explore the reasons for the change.
- Allocate enough funding and resources for departments to sustain support for the community.

The agency continues to expand the use of in-memory analytics. The user community has grown exponentially as well from hundreds to thousands. The adoption of the technology is very high as personnel in various departments have complimented its ease of use and the analytical capabilities it offers with superior performance. What has taken months to process can now be done in hours, which makes this agency very happy. It is striving to be better every day for its country and citizens.

The agency has shared with me the many benefits of using in-memory analytics integrated with the data warehouse.

- Decades of data are now centralized and managed effectively for analytical needs.

- It eliminates the number of data marts and costs of managing these data silos.
- It enables staff to run complex analyses with terabytes of data.
- It provides one platform for all information (via the dashboard) to be shared and consumed.
- Its a access to granular data via the dashboard on mobile devices enables the agency to collect more debt and increase revenue.
- It increases the productivity of the business analysts and users of the information.

INVESTMENT FOR IN-MEMORY ANALYTICS

When I speak to customers about in-memory analytics, one topic that comes up consistently is the investment or cost associated with the hardware and software. Of course, it depends on the vendor and the architecture that you choose to select. Every vendor offers different options when it comes to in-memory analytics. On the hardware side, you will likely need an appliance or a separate server to host the in-memory analytics. The nodes that reside in the appliance or server should be dedicated for in-memory analytics. When sizing the hardware, you should work with the vendor to configure the system appropriately by providing the vendor the following information based on your organization's requirements:

How many total users will have access to the environment?

In this case, the environment refers to the software and the appliance or server that supports in-memory analytics. As users access the data from the data warehouse and lift it into in-memory for analysis, the size of the appliance should be configured correctly to meet the needs of the number of users.

How many concurrent sessions may be running?

In-memory analytics may be used in many concurrent sessions from an enterprise or departmental level. Depending on the size of your organization, consider one or two departments first to have access to in-memory analytics and run concurrent sessions such as in-memory data visualization and domain specific such as data mining.

How many concurrent users are running in-memory analytics?

Customers tend to start with a small group of less than five and slowly expand to thousands. The reason for the initial small group is to test the technology, gain confidence in its ability and performance, and see the value of in-memory analytics. Once it shows success, the number of users tends to grow exponentially. How many users will you log in with a mobile device to access the information?

What is the amount of data that will be lifted into memory from the data warehouse?

The amount of the data determines the number of nodes needed in the appliance or server. Keep in mind that the nodes in the appliance or server are all dedicated to running in-memory analytics. Thus, you will get superior speed and performance for any complex, advanced analytics tasks that are data- and compute-intensive because of the dedicated nodes.

What is the largest size data to be used?

Whether it is in the gigabytes or petabytes, the software and hardware need to be configured to analyze your largest data set. Most of our customers who leverage in-memory analytics are in the petabytes.

Do you know the number of rows and columns of the data being analyzed in-memory?

Most of our customers have thousands to billions of rows and columns of data whether it is customer data, SKUS in retail, or manufacturing parts data.

On the software side, there are solutions that offer in-memory data visualization with deep analytical capabilities. In addition, there are specific domain in-memory analytics packages for data mining, statistics, forecasting, econometrics, text mining, and optimization. If a customer is looking for industry-specific in-memory solution, there are anti-money-laundering, risk, and marketing optimization. Depending on your needs, I advise the customers to adopt one solution and test it out to see if it meets the requirements of your business. Once you have proven it to be successful, you can expand the hardware and adopt additional software packages to extend the use of in-memory analytics.

When selecting an in-memory package, it is essential to ensure that the analytics is well integrated with the data warehouse.

By now, you get a good sense of what is in-memory analytics and what it can do. I tend to compare in-memory analytics to the *sprint stage* while in-database is the *crawl stage*. The next chapter covers Hadoop, which has been a trendy topic in the IT industry for the last few years. Hadoop will be the last piece of the *relay,* and then we will see how in-database, in-memory, and Hadoop fit into the big picture that customers are embracing.

CHAPTER 4
Hadoop

Hadoop is a hot and trendy topic that is growing in popularity as an emerging, modern technology to tackle big data and the increasing amount of data being generated. It is a new approach to manage all of your structured and semi-structured data, analyze, and deliver results. You can find many books, blogs, articles, and websites about Hadoop. In addition, there are many conferences focusing on Hadoop, and many vendors are jumping on the Hadoop bandwagon to develop, integrate, and implement this technology. Customers and prospects are excited because of its open source and claim to be low cost. I will modestly cover Hadoop at a high level in its simplistic form—how it is related to analytics and data management, and how it can fit into your architecture. If your desire is to have a more in-depth understanding of Hadoop, I kindly suggest additional resources from the Internet and software vendors such as Hortonworks or Cloudera. The following topics will be covered in this chapter:

- What is Hadoop?
- Why is Hadoop in the big data environment?
- How does Hadoop fit in the modern architecture?
- What are some best practices?
- What are some use cases and success stories?
- What are the benefits of using Hadoop in big data?

BACKGROUND

The history of Hadoop is fluid. According to my research, the fundamental technology behind Hadoop was invented by Google and had a tremendous amount of influence from Yahoo!. The underlying concept for this technology is to conveniently index and store all the rich textural and structural data being assimilated, analyze the data, and then present noteworthy and actionable results to users. It sounds pretty simple but at that time, in early 2000s, there was nothing in the market to process massive volumes of data (terabytes and beyond) in a distributed environment quickly and efficiently. Yet very little of the information is formatted in the traditional rows and columns of conventional databases. Google's innovative initiative was incorporated into an open source project called Nutch, and then it was spun off in mid-2000 to what is known now as Hadoop. Hadoop is the brain-child of Doug Cutting and Mike Cafarella, who continue to be influential today with open source technology. There are many definitions to what Hadoop is and what it can do. However, I try to use the most simplistic definition. In layman's term, Hadoop is open *source* software to *store* lots of data in a file system and *process* massive volumes of data quickly in a distributed environment. Let's break down what Hadoop provides:

1. *Open source*: Refers to a software or computer program in which the source code is available to the general public for use and/or alteration from its original design.
2. *Store*: Refers to the Hadoop Distributed File System (HDFS), which is a distributed, scalable, and portable file system for storing large files (typically in the range of gigabytes to petabytes) across multiple servers.
3. *Process*: Refers to MapReduce, which is a programming model for parallel processing of large data sets. MapReduce consists of two components:
    a. Map is a method that performs filtering and sorting of data.
    b. Reduce is a method that performs a summary of the data.

To break it down even further, MapReduce coordinates the processing of (big) data by executing the various tasks in parallel across a distributed network of machines and manages all data transfers between the various parts of the system. Figure 4.1 illustrates a simplistic view of the Hadoop architecture, where MR stands for MapReduce.

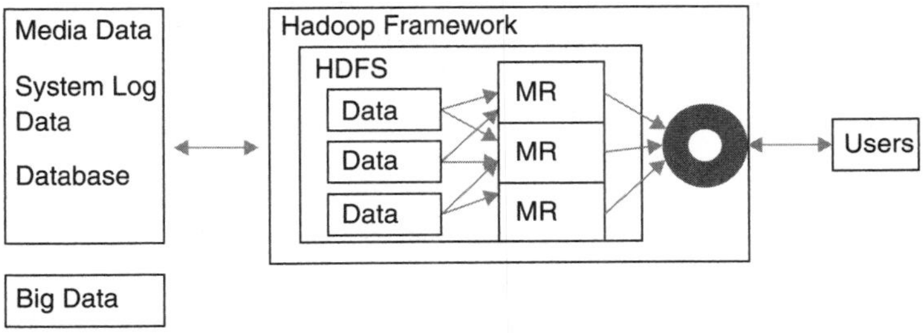

Figure 4.1 Hadoop, HDFS, and MapReduce

Hadoop has grown over the years and is now an ecosystem of products from the open source and vendors communities. Today, Hadoop's framework and ecosystem of technologies are managed and maintained by the nonprofit Apache Software Foundation (ASF), a global community of software developers and contributors.

HADOOP IN THE BIG DATA ENVIRONMENT

Big data is among us, and the amount of data produced and collected is overwhelming. In recent years, due to the arrival of new technologies, devices, and communication types such as social media, the amount of data produced is growing rapidly and exponentially every year. In addition, traditional data is also growing, which I consider is a part of the data ecosystem. Table 4.1 shows the data sources that are considered as big data and the description of the data that you may be collecting for your business.

Table 4.1 Big Data Sources

Type Data	Description
Black Box	Data from airplanes, helicopters, and jets that capture voices and recordings of the flight crew and the performance information of the aircraft.
Power Grid	Power grids data contain information about consumption by a particular node and customer with respect to a base station.
Sensor	Sensor data come from machines or infrastructure such as ventilation equipment, bridges, energy meters, or airplane engines. Can also include meteorological patterns, underground pressure during oil extraction, or a patient's vital statistics during recovery from a medical procedure.
Social Media	Sites such as Facebook, Twitter, Instagram, YouTube, etc., collect a lot of data points from posts, tweets, chats, and videos by millions of people across the globe.
Stock Exchange	The stock exchange holds transaction data about the "buy" and "sell" decisions made on a share of different companies from the customers.
Transport	Transport data encompasses model, capacity, distance, and availability of a car or truck.
Traditional (CRM, ERP, etc.)	Traditional data in rows and columns coming from CRM, ERP, financials about a product, customer, sales, etc.

In addition to the data source mentioned, big data also encompasses everything from call center voice data to genomic data from biological research and medicine. Companies that learn to take advantage of big data will use real-time information from sensors, radio frequency identification, and other identifying devices to understand their business environments at a more granular level, to create new products and services, and to respond to changes in usage patterns as they occur. In the life sciences, such capabilities may pave the way to treatments and cures for threatening diseases.

If you are collecting any or all of the data sources referenced in Table 4.1, then your traditional computing techniques and infrastructure may not be adequate to support the volumes, variety, and velocity of the data being collected. Many organizations may need a new data platform that can handle exploding data volumes, variety, and velocity. They also need a scalable extension for existing IT systems in data warehousing, archiving, and content management. Others may need to finally get business intelligence value out of semi-structured data. Thus, Hadoop was designed and is capable to fulfill these needs with its ecosystem of products. Hadoop is not just a storage platform for big data; it's also a computational platform for analytics. This makes Hadoop ideal for companies that wish to compete on analytics, as well as retain customers, grow accounts, and improve operational excellence via analytics. Many firms believe that, for companies that get it right, big data will be able to unleash new organizational capabilities and value that will increase their bottom line.

USE CASES FOR HADOOP

Hadoop Fits in the Modern Architecture

Before we get into how Hadoop fits into the modern architecture, let's spend a few minutes on the traditional architecture. In the traditional architecture, you likely have a configuration that consists of a data warehouse storing the structured data and data, can be accessed and analyzed using your analytical and/or business intelligence tools. Figure 4.2 shows the typical and traditional architecture.

- *Structured data sources*: These data sources are most likely structured and can include ERP, CRM, legacy systems, financial data,

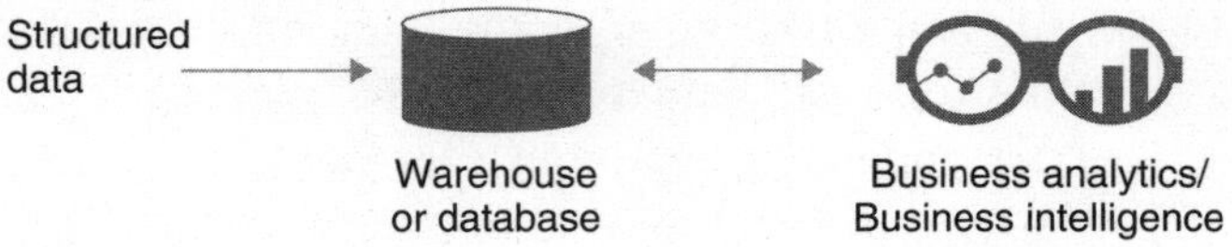

Figure 4.2 Traditional architecture

tech support tickets, and e-commerce. As the data are created and captured, they are stored in an enterprise data warehouse or a relational database.

- *Data warehouse or database*: This is the primary data storage component for the enterprise. It contains a centralized repository for reporting and data analysis. The ETL process is applied to extract, transform, and load the data into the data warehouse that contains cleansed and integrated data. Other forms of storage can be operational warehouse, analytical warehouse, data mart, operational data store, or data warehouse appliance. Data are then accessed with BI and analytical tools for analysis.
- *Business analytics*: This is the analysis and action component in the traditional architecture. Users can access and apply business intelligence and analytics to the data from the warehouse and generate reports for data-driven decisions. Business intelligence and analytic applications may include ad hoc queries, data visualization, descriptive analytics, predictive analytics, online analytical processing (OLAP operational reporting), and prescriptive analytics.

A data warehouse is good at providing consistent, integrated, and accurate data to the users. They can deliver in minutes the summaries, counts, and lists that make up the most common elements of business analytics. The combination of business analytics and massive parallel processing of a data warehouse provides much of the self-service data access to users as well as interactivity. Providing self-service capability is a huge benefit in itself; the ability to interact with the data can teach the user more about the business and can produce new insights.

Another advantage of the warehouse is concurrency. Concurrency in a data warehouse ranges from tens to thousands of people simultaneously accessing the querying the system. The mass parallel processing engine behind the database supports this capability with a superior level of performance and efficiency.

HADOOP ARCHITECTURE

As your business evolves, the data warehouse may not meet the requirements of your organization. Organizations have information needs that are not completely served by a data warehouse. The needs are driven as much by the maturity of the data use in business as they are by new technology.

For example, the relational database at the center of the data warehouse is ideal for data processing to what can be done via SQL. Thus, if the data cannot be processed via SQL, then it limits the analysis of the new data source that is not in row or column format. Other data sources that do not fit nicely in the data warehouse include text, images, audio, and video, all of which are considered as semi-structured data. Thus, this is where Hadoop enters the architecture.

Hadoop is a family of products (Hadoop Distributed File System (HDFS), MapReduce, Pig, Hive, HBase, Mahout, Cassandra, YARN, Ambari, Avro, Chukwa, and Zookeeper), each with different and multiple capabilities. Please visit www.apache.org for details on these products. These products are available as native open source from Apache Software Foundation (ASF) and the software vendors.

Once the data are stored in Hadoop, the big data applications can be used to analyze the data. Figure 4.3 shows a simple stand-alone Hadoop architecture.

- *Semi-structured data sources*: The semi-structured data cannot be stored in a relational database (in column/row format). These data sources include email, social data, XML data, videos, audio

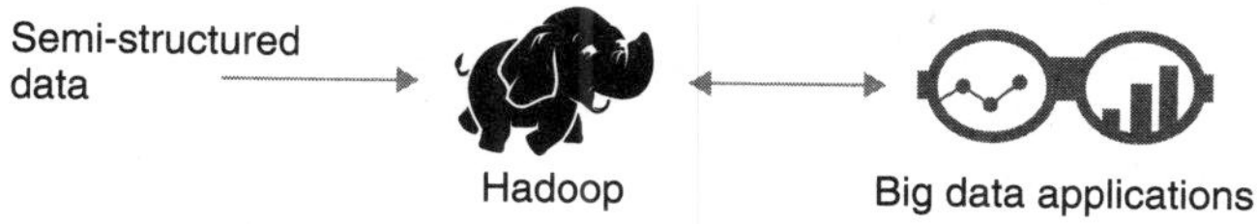

Figure 4.3 Hadoop architecture

files, photos, GPS, satellite images, sensor data, spreadsheets, web log data, mobile data, RFID tags, and PDF docs.

- *Hadoop*: The Hadoop Distributed File System (HDFS), which is the data storage component of the open source Apache Hadoop project, is ideal for collecting the semi-data structured sources. (However, it can also host structured data as well). For this example, it is a simple architecture to capture all of the semi-structured data. Hadoop HDFS is designed to run on less expensive commodity hardware and is able to scale out quickly and inexpensively across a farm of servers.

  MapReduce is a key component of Hadoop. It is the resource management and processing component of Hadoop and also allows programmers to write code that can process large volumes of data. For instance, a programmer can use MapReduce to locate friends or determine the number of contacts in a social network application, or process web access log to analyze web traffic volume and patterns. In addition, MapReduce can process the data where it resides (in HDFS) instead of moving it around, as is sometimes the case in a traditional data warehouse system. It also comes with a built-in recovery system—so if one machine goes down, MapReduce knows where to go to get another copy of the data. Although MapReduce processing is fast when compared to more traditional methods, its jobs must be run in batch mode. This has proven to be a limitation for organizations that need to process data more frequently and/or closer to real time. The good news is that with the release of Hadoop 2.0, the resource management functionality has been packaged separately (it's called YARN) so that MapReduce doesn't get bogged down and can stay focused on processing big data.

- *Big data applications*: This is the analysis and action component using data from Hadoop HDFS. These are the applications, tools, and utilities that have been natively built for users to access, interact, analyze, and make decisions using data in Hadoop and other nonrelational storage systems. It does not include traditional BI/analytics applications or tools that have been extended to support Hadoop.

Since the inception of Hadoop, there is a lot of noise and hype in the market as to what Hadoop can or cannot do. It is definitely not a silver bullet to solve all data management and analytical issues. Keep in mind that Hadoop is an ecosystem of products and provides multipurpose functions to manage and analyze big data. It is good at certain things and has shortcomings as well:

- *Not a database*: A database provides many functions that help to manage the data. Hadoop has HDFS, which is a distributed file system and lacks the database functions such as indexing, random access to data, support for standard SQL, and query optimization. As Hadoop matures and evolves, these functions will likely be part of the ecosystem. For now, you may consider HBase over HDFS to provide some DBMS functionality. Another option is Hive, which provides an SQL-like interface to manage data stored in Hadoop.
- *No multi-temperature data*: The frequency at which data are accessed—often described as its "temperature"—can affect the performance and capability of the warehouse. Hadoop lacks mature query optimization and the ability to place "hot" and "cold" data on a variety of storage devices with different levels of performance. Thus, Hadoop is often complemented with a DBMS that processes the data on Hadoop and moves results to the data warehouse.
- *Lacks user interface*: Users who prefer a user interface for ease of use may not find it with Hadoop. This is one big drawback from customer's feedback. However, many vendors are creating applications to access data from Hadoop with a user interface to fill this gap.
- *Deep learning curve*: From talking to customers, there is a deep learning curve since it is an emerging technology and subject matter experts are few and far between. Once you have learned

Hadoop, the writing of code can be very tedious, time consuming, and costly. Because it is open source, the reliability and stability of the environment can create issues.

- *Limited data manipulation*: Joining data is a common practice to prepare data for analysis. For simple joins, Hadoop offers tools to accommodate those needs. However, for complex joins and SQL, it is not efficient. This process will require extensive programing, which requires time and resources from your organization.
- *Data governance and integrity*: A database or a data warehouse has the ACID properties (atomicity, consistency, isolation, durability) guarantee, which assures that the database transactions are processed with integrity and can be governed. This can impose a challenge for organizations to ensure the integrity of their analyses and results.
- *Lacks security*: Hadoop lacks security features common in RDBMSs, such as row- and column-level security, and it provides minimal user-level controls, authentication options, and encryption.

For the above reasons, I highly recommend integrating Hadoop with your data warehouse. The combination of Hadoop and the data warehouse offers the best of both worlds: managing structured and semi-structured data and optimizing performance for analysis. More scenarios and explanations will be described in the next chapter when I bring all of the elements together.

Now that you know what Hadoop can do, let's shift our focus on some of the best practices for Hadoop.

BEST PRACTICES

As I talk to customers about Hadoop, they share some dos and don'ts based on their experience. Keep in mind that there will be many more best practices as the technology matures into the mainstream and is implemented.

Start small and expand

Every organization has many projects, and you rely heavily on technology to solve your business needs. You have probably heard to focus on a project that gives you the big bang for your buck. For Hadoop, identify a small project with an immediate need. Too many times I have witnessed projects fail in companies due to the level of complexity, lack of resources, and high expenses. Selecting a small project to get started allows the IT and business staffs to become familiar with the interworking of this emerging technology. The beauty of Hadoop is that it allows you to start small and add nodes as you go.

Consider commodity server

Many database vendors offer commercial Hadoop distribution with their appliance or hardware. This offer can easily be integrated with the current data warehouse infrastructure. However, I work with customers who adopted commodity server to control costs and work within their budgets. Commodity servers are simply a bunch of disks with single power supplies to store data. Adopting commodity servers will require resources to be trained to manage and gain knowledge of how Hadoop works on commodity. Adopting commodity can be an alternative but may not be suited for your environment.

Monitor the infrastructure

As mentioned earlier, Hadoop is an ecosystem and there are many parts with multipurpose functions. These moving parts relate to the data and management level, and it is recommended to monitor the infrastructure. By monitoring the infrastructure, you can detect problems before they occur and know problems immediately when issues arise such as disk capacity or failure.

Develop a data integration process

With any data management technology, the process of integrating data is very critical. Hadoop can store all data, both structured and semi-structured. Hadoop allows you to populate the data and you can define the structure at a later time. Ensuring that the data are standardized, named, and located up front can help to make it easier for analysis. Many customers use Hadoop as a staging area for all of the data collected. The integration process enhances reliability and integrity of the data.

Compression is your companion

IT has had a love–hate relationship with compression over the years. This is also true with a RDBMS. Compression saves space, but performance can be impacted when it comes to the production systems. Hadoop, by contrast, flourishes on and leverages the use of compression, and it can increase storage usage by many folds.

Enforce a multiple environment infrastructure

Just like any other IT project, I always advise our customers to build multiple environments (Development, Test, Production) infrastructure. Not only is this a common best practice but it is also vital because of the nature of Hadoop and its nature as an emerging technology. Each project within the Hadoop Ecosystem is constantly changing and having a nonproduction environment to test upgrades and new functionality is critical. Customers who have one environment tend to pay the price when the upgrades are not successful.

Preserve separate functions of master and worker nodes

Master nodes and worker nodes play two extremely different roles. Master nodes oversee and coordinate the data storage function (HDFS). They should be placed on servers that have fully redundant features such as redundant array of independent disks (RAID) and with multiple power adapters. Master nodes also play well in a virtual environment due to the extra redundancy this provides. Worker nodes on the other hand are the work horses of the cluster and do all the dirty work of storing the data and running the computations. Therefore, these worker nodes need to be dedicated solely to this important function. If you mix these nodes on the same server, it usually leads to undesirable results and unwanted issues.

Keep it simple and don't overbuild

Your first Hadoop project should be small and simple to build. You may get excited and get carried away over building your first Hadoop cluster. The costs of hardware and software may be low initially, but it's important to only build to what your initial requirements require to solve a business problem. You might find the specifications of the servers you selected need to be modified based on the results and performance of your initial project. As they say, it's easier to add than to take away.

Leverage the open source community

Every project has its hiccups. When things go wrong, you have a local or online community. Hadoop is driven by the open source community and there is a very good chance the problem you are having is just a quick click away using online search engine. The Hadoop ecosystem continues to mature and the community is a great resource to conquer your issues.

Implement some of these best practices

There is a lot of hype to what Hadoop is or is not. You may consider Hadoop as a big data storage—*data lake*—where you can just store all of your data for the time being and deal with it later. I highly recommend that you instill some of these best practices, and develop documentation and rules for the project before it gets out of control. Once it gets out of control, it will be costly to fix and time consuming, which can delay the completion of the project.

Now that you are aware of the technology and some of the best practices, let's check out some of the benefits, use cases, and success stories.

BENEFITS OF HADOOP

In the previous section, customers who implemented Hadoop saw business value and IT benefits. The benefits that follow are the most common ones from talking to customers. As the technology becomes more mature, the benefits will continue to grow in business and IT.

Store and process big data of any kind quickly

Hadoop is great at storing and processing massive amounts of data of any kind, which are inclusive of structured and semi-structured data. In big data, the 3 V(s)—volume, variety, and velocity—constantly increase and continue to exponentially grow, especially from social media and the Internet of Things (IoT).

Flexibility with data structure and preprocessing

You will likely need to structure a relational database or data warehouse in columns and rows to be in an integrated format before you can store it. This preprocess can be time consuming and resource intensive. With Hadoop, there is no preprocessing of the data, you can simply store as much data as you want and determine how to use it later. In addition to the structured data, the flexibility extends to the semi-structured data such as text, images, and videos.

Fault tolerance

With fault tolerance, your data and application processing are protected against any hardware failure. If a node or server goes down, your jobs are automatically redirected to other nodes within the network to make sure the distributed computing does not fail. All data and their duplicates are stored automatically so you don't lose any of your strategic assets.

Scalable

Hadoop's distributed computing model processes large amount of data fast. You may have terabytes or petabytes of data that need to be processed, analyzed, and managed. When you need more compute capacity, you can simply add more nodes to the server to get more processing power.

Low cost

I mention the low cost of the commodity server that you can use to run Hadoop and store large quantities of data. In addition, Hadoop is open source software and its framework is free. This benefit is the most popular among customers who consider and adopt Hadoop.

USE CASES AND SUCCESS STORIES

A recent "Best Practices Report" conducted by The Data Warehousing Institute (TDWI) revealed some interesting findings for the usage of Hadoop across all industries.[1] The report consisted of several surveys and one of them asked the participants to name the most useful application of Hadoop if their organization were to adopt and employ it. Following is a snapshot from the survey.

46%: Data warehouse extensions
In other words, Hadoop complements the data warehouse or RDBMS. It is used to store semi-structured data while the data warehouse is storing the traditional structured data.

46%: Data exploration and discovery
Hadoop is an ideal platform for data exploration and discovery to know what data you have and understand its potential business value before it gets analyzed. Once you know what you have, you can develop the data for analytics.

39%: Data staging area for data warehousing and data integration
Instead of applying the ETL process at the data warehouse platform, you can apply the data integration process to stage or prepare the data for loading. This is another option for customers to manage the data and only load the data into the data warehouse as needed. Otherwise, the data can stay in Hadoop.

36%: Data lakes
Data lakes are considered as large repository for all data types. For example, you can store all your raw data as it is generated and captured and decide what you want to keep at later time.

36%: Queryable archive for nontraditional data (web logs, sensor, social, etc.)
Like the data warehouse is an archiving platform for traditional or structured data, Hadoop can be the archiving platform for semi-structured data or the nontraditional data sources. It is a less

expensive option to storing data that may no longer relevant or outdated.

33%: Computational platform and sandbox for advanced analytics

A sandbox is defined as an area to explore and examine new ideas and possibilities by combining new data with existing data to create experimental designs and ad-hoc queries without interrupting the production environment. This is ideal to test and experiment the new functionality such as in-database or in-memory analytics.

In my research, there are many public-use cases and success stories that you can find on the web by simply searching for them. It is no surprise that Google and Yahoo! leverage Hadoop because they were both involved in the development and maturation of this technology. In my research, I discovered a plethora of companies across industries using Hadoop. Many of the use cases are very similar in nature and share a common theme—support of semi-structured data using HDFS and MapReduce.

Global Online and Social Networking Website

Our first success story comes from an American corporation that provides online social networking services. With tens of millions of users and more than a billion page views every day, this company accumulates massive amounts of data and ends up with terabytes of data to process. It is probably more so than your typical organization, especially considering the amount of media it consumes. This corporation leverages Hadoop since its inception to explore the data and improve user experience.

Background

One of the challenges that this company has faced is developing a scalable way of storing and processing all massive amounts of data. Collecting and analyzing historical data is a very big part of this company so that it can improve the user experience.

Years ago, it began playing around with the idea of implementing Hadoop to handle its massive data consumption and aggregation.

In the early days of considering Hadoop, it was questionable whether importing some interesting data sets into a relatively small cluster of servers was feasible. Developers were quickly excited to learn that processing big data sets was possible with MapReduce programming model where this capability was not previously possible due to their massive computational requirements.

Exploring Data with Hadoop

Hadoop is a big hit at this organization. It has multiple Hadoop clusters deployed now—with the biggest having about 2,500 central processing unit (cpu) cores and 1 petabyte of disk space. This company is loading over 250 gigabytes of compressed data (over 2 terabytes uncompressed) into the Hadoop file system every day and has hundreds of jobs running daily against these data sets. The list of projects that are using this infrastructure has increased tremendously—from those generating mundane statistics about site usage, to others being used to fight spam and determine application quality. A majority of the engineering staff has played with and run Hadoop at this company.

There are a number of reasons for the rapid adoption of Hadoop. First, developers are free to write MapReduce programs in the language of their choice. Second, engineers have embraced SQL as a familiar paradigm to address and operate on large data sets. Most data stored in Hadoop's file system are published as tables. Developers and engineers can explore the schemas and data of these tables much like they would do with a relational database management system (RDBMS). A combination of MapReduce and SQL can be very powerful to retrieve and process semi-structured and structured data.

At the corporate level, it is incredibly important that they use the information generated by and from their users to make decisions about improvements to the product and services. Hadoop has enabled them to make better use of the data at their disposal.

Global Consumer Transaction Company: Data Landing Zone

Our next customer is a global leader in consumer transaction technologies, turning everyday interactions with businesses into exceptional experiences. With the software, hardware, and portfolio of services, this company makes nearly 550 million transactions possible daily.

This company's motto is to help their customers respond to the demand for fast, easy, and convenient transactions with intuitive self-service and assisted-service options. But what they do goes beyond niche technologies or markets. Their solutions help businesses around the world increase revenue, build loyalty, reach new customers, and lower their costs of operations.

By continually learning about—and pioneering—how the world interacts and transacts, this global leader is helping companies not only reach their goals, but also change the way all of us shop, eat, travel, bank, and connect. They include thousands of banks and retailers that depend on tens of thousands of self-service kiosks, point-of-sale (POS) terminals, ATMs (automated teller machines), and barcode scanners, among other equipment.

Traditional Approach

In the traditional architecture, this customer could only collect a snapshot of data, which limited the accuracy of its predictive models. For example, the company might collect snapshots from a sampling of ATMs (perhaps once-daily performance data) where the real need is to collect the entire set.

In addition, this company needed to avoid downtime for its clients at all costs. The traditional architecture could not collect millions of records with many data sources and analyze it in a timeline manner to predict the likelihood of a device for preventative maintenance, replacement, or upgrades. Having downtime means that their clients would not be able to operate, and it hurts the reputation of the company. Furthermore, it could not store real-time performance data from every deployed device in banks and retailers and, therefore, was unable to analyze them to detect and prevent downtime for these devices. This process could not be done with the traditional architecture.

Hadoop: A Landing Zone for Data Exploration

As mentioned in Chapter 1, Hadoop is used in the data exploration phase in the analytical data life cycle. It is a common use for Hadoop to be a landing zone for all data, to explore what you have before you apply any analysis to the data.

This customer considered Hadoop to be a landing zone for all data, as Hadoop is good at storing both structured and semi-structured data. Hadoop provides the technology to efficiently and effectively store large amounts of data—that includes data that they are not sure yet how they will use.

To resolve the downtime issue mentioned previously, it is leveraging Hadoop as a "data lake" where it has the capacity to gather and store real-time performance data from every deployed device in banks and retailers. This type of data is not only big in millions of records, but also in the rate or velocity that it is collected. From the data, this company can create rich predictive models using advanced analytics to detect and prevent downtime. It is able to analyze the entire set of data, not just a subset; it is able to build predictive models. For example, the data lake built on Hadoop can monitor every ATM machine it manufactures and develop data models to predict its failure. Fortunately, the downtime is few and far between, due to how big data is collected and analyzed.

Another use for Hadoop is collecting a new data source such as the telephony data to analyze the use of tele-presence devices worldwide. When communications are done between offices, this customer is able to determine the most efficient path and advise where to put telephony equipment in the network. This is purely operational use of the data, and a business analyst responsible for financial analysis of the product's portfolio may never considered looking at retail service calls. With Hadoop and collecting the telephony data, this company is able to expand the scope of the query and root cause analysis to see how a collocated printer, for example, might be shared between a point of sale device, an ATM, and a self-checkout device. The ability to leverage all the data in one place for analytics across lines of business and sharing analytical results creates a culture of openness and of information sharing.

Let's examine another customer success story using Hadoop.

Global Payment Services Company: Hadoop Combining Structured and Semi-Structured Data

Our next success story comes from a global payment services company that provides consumers and businesses with fast, reliable, and convenient ways to send and receive money around the world, to send payments, and to purchase money orders. With a combined network of over 500,000 agent locations in 200 countries and territories and over 100,000 ATMs and kiosks, this customer completed 255 million consumer-to-consumer transactions worldwide, moving $85 billion of principal between consumers and 484 million business payments. Its core business includes

- Retail, online, ATM, and mobile consumer-to-consumer money transfers
- Stored-value solutions, including prepaid cards and money orders
- Consumer bill payments
- Cross-border business payments for small- and medium-sized enterprises

Background

This customer has been collecting structured data for many years. With the popularity of the Internet and web services, its customers are leveraging the online services to send money to other people, pay bills, and buy or reload prepaid debit cards, or find the locations of agents for in-person services. To give you a sense of the volume, more than 70 million users tapped into their services online, in person, or by phone, and the company said it averaged 29 transactions per second across 200 countries and territories. Thus, web data were growing fast and needed to be captured and analyzed for business needs. Log-based clickstream data about user activity from the website were captured in semi-structured nonrelational formats, and then got mixed and integrated with the relational data to give this customer a true view of their customer activity and engagements. All of the structured and semi-structured data were considered as funnels for a data analysis pipeline. With the traditional infrastructure, only the structured data was captured, integrated, and analyzed. Now, there is a need to integrate large amounts of web data into the corporate workflow to provide a holistic view of its operations.

The current infrastructure was unable to accommodate the business needs. The amount of data was so huge that analyzing it was a challenge and getting answers from massive amounts of data was very difficult. Because data are touched and shared across the enterprise, data scientists, business analysts, and marketing personnel were unable to rely on the existing technology for their data management and analytical needs.

Hadoop: Part of the Enterprise Architecture

At this money-transfer and payment services company, incorporating Hadoop into its enterprise operations also meant successfully integrating large amounts of web data into the corporate workflow. Significant work was required to make new forms of data readily accessible and usable by many staff members—data scientists, business analysts, marketing, and sales. Hadoop is the center of a self-service business intelligence and analytics platform that consists of a variety of others systems and software components. Hadoop feeds these applications the data needed since it is collecting all of semi-structured data.

This customer is adding data from mobile devices to its Hadoop environment and complements it with online data from the Internet. Once the streams of data, structured and semi-structured, are collected, it is parsed and prepared for analysis using a collection of technologies:

- Data integration tool to integrate and transform the data
- Data warehousing technology to store the structured data
- Analytics tools for analysis from Hadoop and the data warehouse

The Hadoop system continues to grow in importance at this global payment company. The enterprise architecture that includes Hadoop is expanding into risk analysis and compliance with financial regulation, anti-money laundering, and other financial crimes. Hadoop is widely used and crucial to the analytics process.

A COLLECTION OF USE CASES

- A U.S.-based casino-entertainment company is using a new Hadoop environment to define customer segments and develop specific marketing campaigns tailored to each of those segments. With Hadoop, the new environment has reduced processing time for key jobs from about 6 hours to 45 minutes. The reduced processing time allows the casino to run faster and more accurate data analysis. In addition, it has improved customer experiences and increased security for meeting payment card industry (PCI) and other standards. The customer can now process more than 3 million records per hour, much more than what it could do without Hadoop.

- A healthcare technology company has built an enterprise data hub using Hadoop to create a more complete view of any patient, condition, or trend. Hadoop is helping this company and its clients monitor more than one million patients every day. In addition, it is helping to detect the likelihood that a patient has the potentially fatal bloodstream infection, sepsis, with a much greater accuracy than was previously possible.
- A relationship-minded online dating website uses Hadoop to analyze a massive volume and variety of data. The technology is helping this company to deliver new matches to millions of people every day, and the new environment accommodates more complex analyses to create more personalized results and improve the chances of relationship success.

There is no question that big data is here, and organizations are spinning in an expanding wealth of data that is either too voluminous or not structured enough to be managed and analyzed through traditional means and approaches. Hadoop is a technology that can complement your traditional architecture to support the semi-structured data that you are collecting. Big data has prompted organizations to rethink and restructure from the business and IT sides. Managing data has always been in the forefront, and analytics has been more of an afterthought. Now, it seems big data has brought analytics to the forefront along with data management. Organizations need to realize that the world we live in is changing, and so is the data. It is prudent for businesses to recognize these changes and react quickly and intelligently to gain the competitive advantage and the upper hand. The new paradigm is no longer stability; it is now agility and discovery. As the volume of data explodes, organizations will need a platform to support new data sources and analytic capability. As big data evolves, the Hadoop architecture will develop into a modern information ecosystem that is a network of internal and external services continuously allocating information, optimizing data-driven decisions, communicating results, and generating new, strategic insights for businesses.

In the next chapter, we will bring it all together with Hadoop with the data warehouse leveraging in-database analytics and in-memory analytics in an integrated architecture.

ENDNOTE

1. The Data Warehouse Institute, "Best Practices Report: Hadoop for the Enterprise," *TDWI Onsite Education* (April 1, 2015), https://tdwi.org/research/2015/03/best-practices-report-hadoop-for-the-enterprise.aspx?tc=page0.

CHAPTER 5

Bringing It All Together

In Chapter 2, we discussed in-database processing and its value of applying analytics where the data reside. In Chapter 3, we explained in-memory analytics and how data could be lifted in-memory for game-changing results. In Chapter 4, we introduced Hadoop and how it can fit into the data management and analytical landscape. Each of the previous chapters combined is like a running a relay, and we tie it all together in this chapter to help you through the stages—crawl, walk, and sprint. Now, let's bring all of the components together (in-database, in-memory, Hadoop) into what I call a collaborative data architecture so that your organization can effectively run a seamless relay to conquering big data management and analytics.

This chapter will cover the following topics:

- How in-database analytics, in-memory analytics, and Hadoop are complementary in a collaborative data architecture
- Use cases and customer success stories
- The benefits of an integrated data management and analytic architecture

BACKGROUND

Historically, many companies have adopted one data management system to store all their data in the form of an enterprise data warehouse or departmental data mart. This single-system architecture may have met the business requirements when it is mainly structured data. The analytics and reporting applications can access the data and analyze and deliver results to management when requested. As time progressed, three things have evolved:

1. Data volumes are growing and organizations are purchasing new hardware/software to accommodate the growth.
2. Business analytics and reporting are generated in near real time, which puts an extreme burden on querying performance.
3. Analytics are becoming more complex with more data to analyze, variables to consider, and data models to execute for data-driven decisions.

The analytics workloads involve extensive calculations and are both compute-intensive and read-intensive, which can place a heavy burden on the data warehouse. The process normally requires retrieving the entire data sets and not just a subset. Most analytic workloads are executed in a batch mode, and the results from these workloads are fed to various downstream applications such as business intelligence, reporting, and/or visualization.

As the analytic workloads grow bigger with more complex computations and many more variables to consider, organizations are stretching their single data warehouse environment to its capacity. Businesses have three options:

1. Purchase additional servers or hardware to expand the use of the data warehouse.
2. Add workload-specific hardware that is tied to the data warehouse such as a data mart.
3. Decide what data to keep in the data warehouse and offload nonessential data to other platforms.

Combining these options will give you the optimal environment for existing use cases as well as new use cases to meet the business requirements for data-intensive analytical projects. However, having one data management system might not be the best fit to manage the structured data and semi-structured data.

COLLABORATIVE DATA ARCHITECTURE

Your current data warehouse may scale well to support complex analytics and data models and access from hundreds of users with varying workloads in a rigorously controlled, highly governed, and managed environment, but there are classes or data types that are not likely going to benefit from having that data residing in the data warehouse. You may need to recognize that the enterprise data warehouse may not always be the ideal place for certain classes of data. For example, your data warehouse might support semi-structured data, log files, or streaming sensor outputs to be stored in the form of binary large object (BLOBs), but placing them there might not provide any analytic lift for the statisticians or data scientists. Data types like BLOBs are very capable of storing virtually any random content, but if your end goal is to support parsing, text analytics, and keyword lookups, then perhaps storing them in another platform may be more suitable and preferable for optimal use.

To accommodate the various classes and types of data, the collaborative data architecture is ideal for integrating data management and analytics within a unified platform, as shown in Figure 5.1. Most likely, your data sources come from your ERP, CRM, images, audio, visual, logs, text, web, and social media. As the data sources are captured, they can be stored in any or all of the three platforms shown.

Collaborative Data Architecture provides three distinct, purpose-built data management platforms, each integrated with the others, intended for specialized needs for your data.

Staging Warehouse

The *staging warehouse* platform is intended to be an economical platform to capture and store all your data types. This data may not be

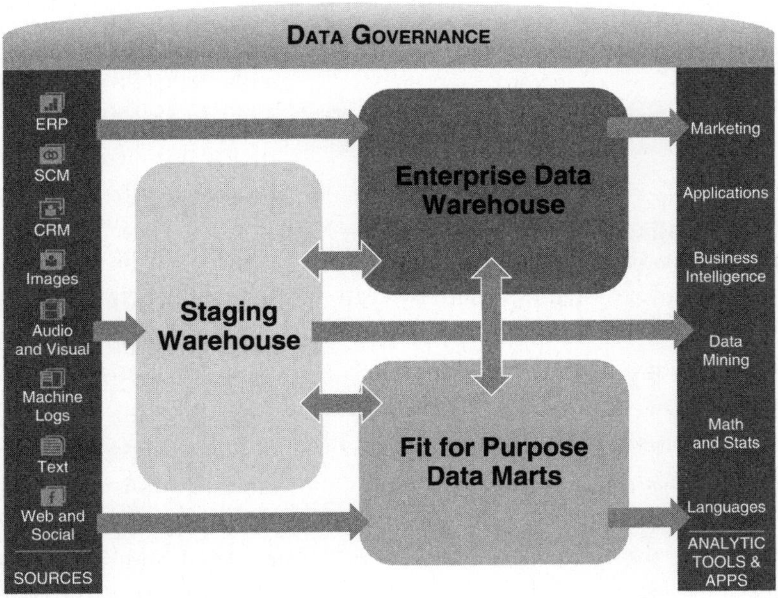

Figure 5.1 Collaborative data architecture

fully structured, and do not yet need to be accessed for operational reporting across the enterprise. Frequently, the platform is used to collect sets of enormous files, like web logs, machine sensor outputs, or even web log outputs, all of which have some analytic value to them, and semi-structured data. Most importantly, it just needs to be stored in a large clustered file system.

This platform is ideal for supporting highly flexible data capture and staging for all data sources, including structured and semi-structured. For example, you can leverage the Hadoop technology for pre-processing of large volumes of data and preparing the data to be stored in the data warehouse or data mart, or be used by any of the applications such as analytics, business intelligence, or marketing.

Fit for Purpose Data Mart

This platform is a subset of the data warehouse that is usually purposely built for a specific department, group, business team, or line of business. Because it is a subset of the data warehouse, the data mart improves end-user response time by allowing users to have access to the specific type of data they need.

The *fit for purpose data mart* could be intended for specific analytic processing, but organized into functional areas such as marketing, operations research, sales operations, and so on. In this case, there's a trade-off, where we are dropping some of the user concurrency requirements in exchange for high levels of analytic flexibility.

For example, customers leverage a data mart for just demand forecasting. All of the data residing in this data mart can be used for a selected group of data modelers and data scientists who build statistical data models to anticipate supply and demand for products and services. Another example is in the pharmaceutical industry where a data mart is created for a specific drug development analysis. There are many variables and data points for analysis to bring a product to market. In the pharmaceutical industry, strict standards and regulations are in place and must be followed before a drug is available to the consumers. Thus, this data mart is highly governed and only accessible by a small group of data scientists for analytics and modeling purposes.

Enterprise Data Warehouse

This platform is for delivering strategic and operational analytics throughout your organization, so users from across the company can access a single source of consistent, centralized, and integrated data.

The *enterprise data warehouse* is targeted at rigorous, highly structured, "ready for prime time" data that can be used by business and analytic users across all departments or enterprise. The data warehouse addresses enterprise data readiness concerns, not only with the ability to scale to support more users, wider range of user applications, or larger volumes of data, but also to anticipate potential failures, keep running in the state of problems, and provide management and monitoring environment to ensure that the environment continually supports data access from around the business. It is ideally suited for modeled and integrated data to support end-to-end optimization and operationalization.

Many customers already utilize an enterprise data warehouse to gather data from multiple operational data sources that integrate together to provide a "single version of the truth." The integrated data in the data warehouse possibly feeds hundreds of downstream applications and thousands of business users. However, much if not all of the data are generally relational; organized into tables, rows, and columns; and accessible by SQL. Depending on the data maturity that you may be working with, other platforms may be better suited, such as the staging warehouse or the fit for purpose data mart.

For larger companies, they may utilize the different aspects of the collaborative data architecture side by side, each with a special purpose perspective on the end-to-end data life cycle, evolving and maturing data from its "staged" landing area on Hadoop, right up to the "ready for action" enterprise data warehouse environment.

The ultimate goal for the collaborative data architecture is to enable organizations to access and analyze all their data to make smarter decisions and develop a new, data-driven approach to improving their business and the bottom line. The ability to apply analytics and to deliver deeper insights about your customers, operations, and services can deliver a unique competitive advantage. Let's examine in the next section how data and analytics can be managed in the different scenarios.

SCENARIOS FOR THE COLLABORATIVE DATA ARCHITECTURE

In Chapter 4, I illustrated the basic architecture of how structured data can be stored in the data warehouse and semi-structured data can be stored in Hadoop. Let's expand on the use and tie it to the collaborative data architecture.

In our first scenario, we use Hadoop as a staging platform for your enterprise data warehouse, as shown in Figure 5.2.

If your organization is just collecting structured data, this scenario can be ideal for you. In this setup, it is a simple case of capturing and managing structured data and integrating with Hadoop. Hadoop can be used as a data staging warehouse or platform to load data into your enterprise data warehouse. Instead of staging the data at the data warehouse level, you can apply the data integration process at the Hadoop platform. According to The Data Warehousing Institute (TDWI) "Best Practices Report" on Hadoop, 39 percent of the participants surveyed indicated that they use Hadoop for their data staging area for data warehousing and data integration.[1]

As mentioned in Chapter 4, Hadoop comes with Hadoop Distributed File System (HDFS) and MapReduce. You can leverage MapReduce by writing some code to bring the data into HDFS, transform it, and then load the integrated data into the enterprise data warehouse. In this situation, you can choose the data that you want to transform and load into the data warehouse, and the remaining

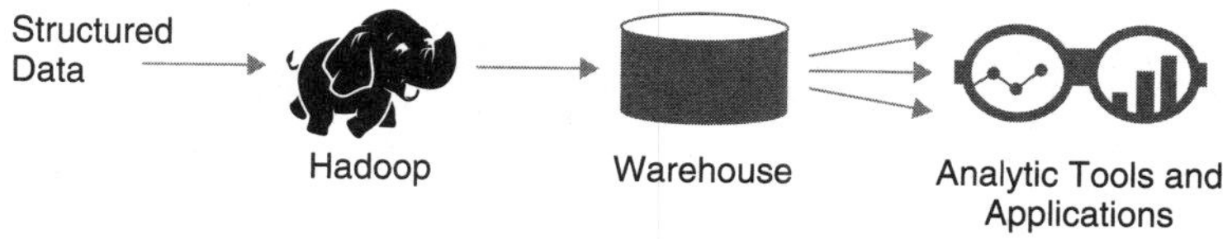

Figure 5.2 Hadoop as a staging warehouse for your structured data

data can be kept in Hadoop until it is ready to be transformed. This approach has several benefits:

Distribute the processing power

It can be challenging to get all of your ETL (Extraction, Transformation, and Load) jobs to complete in a timely manner with higher volumes of data. If that is your case, you may want to consider leveraging Hadoop to offload some of this tedious work to the Hadoop platform. Typically, you process the data by applying the ETL functions at the data warehouse platform. With Hadoop in the mix, it can handle some of the data manipulation and preparation for you. Hadoop can be the staging platform and can free up the resources from your enterprise data warehouse. Data can be processed, transformed, and then loaded into the enterprise data warehouse quicker so that the downstream applications can access and analyze the data.

Cost

Over the years, the cost of storage has dropped significantly, and Hadoop can be a great medium for this purpose. All your raw data can be stored and kept in one place. You can easily manage the data, process it when ready, and load it into the enterprise data warehouse for analysis. Since Hadoop keeps a copy of the raw and transformed data, having an alternative low-cost option is valuable for managing data growth.

If your company is capturing semi-structured data sources and you want to integrate them with your structured data, then Hadoop can help to manage all your data sources. In Figure 5.3, consider Hadoop to be your data lake for all your data sources as they are captured.

The infrastructure in Figure 5.3 is very similar to Figure 5.2, but in this instance, you are incorporating semi-structured data into the mix. Hadoop can act as your data lake—a temporary data storage for all your data sources. In this circumstance, you can integrate the data that is not currently available in your enterprise data warehouse. For example, some of your structured data sources coming into Hadoop may not be integrated into your enterprise data warehouse.

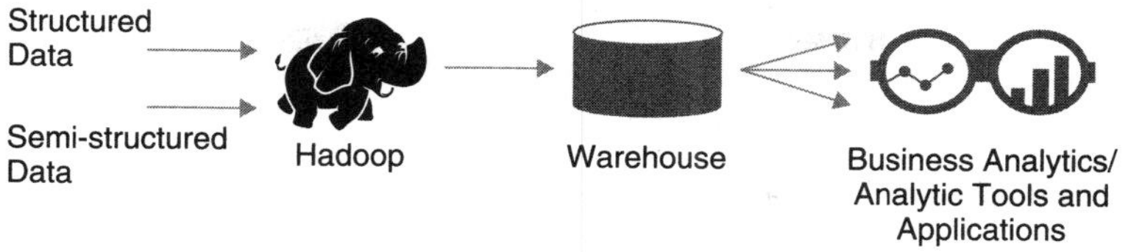

Figure 5.3 Hadoop as a data lake

In addition, you can now include the semi-structured data to provide additional insight about your customers, products, and services. Because Hadoop can store any data source, it can be complementary to the enterprise data warehouse. According to the TDWI "Best Practices Report," 46 percent of the respondents indicate that they use Hadoop as a complementary extension of a data warehouse.[2] In the same report, 36 percent of the participants say that they use Hadoop as a data lake. You should consider this architecture if you want to integrate structured and semi-structured data in one location.

In this situation, your enterprise data warehouse is the center of your universe and the key component for your analytics applications and business intelligence tools to access for analysis. This arrangement is geared toward organizations that want to keep the enterprise data warehouse as the de facto system of data. Hadoop is used as the data lake to capture all data sources and process and integrate them before they get loaded into the enterprise data warehouse.

Benefits for this scenario include the following:

Data lake advantage

The data lake can capture all of your data sources at a lower cost. Your data warehouse can be used for critical mission analysis while the data lake can store all noncritical data. You can keep what data you want and flush what you do not want to keep, while the data warehouse is for cleansed and integrated data for your enterprise.

Complementary use of Hadoop

Hadoop extends traditional data warehouse infrastructure to support more data and offload some of the work from the data warehouse to be more efficient.

Highly governed environment

Because all of your data are stored in one place and leverage the enterprise data warehouse for all analyses, data governance is at its highest. All users access the data from the warehouse to apply analytics or reporting for the business needs.

In our next scenario, the environment gets a bit more complex to provide you the flexibility for the enterprise and departmental needs, as shown in Figure 5.4.

Let's expand the setup to include a data mart for data exploration and discovery. In this scenario, you can use Hadoop as the landing/staging platform and exploit the strengths of Hadoop and the data warehouse. The concept of the data warehouse has existed for over 30 years and this infrastructure shifts the data management paradigm is a major way. As organizations have spent years in resources and financial support to build their enterprise data warehouse, Hadoop literally pops up as this emerging technology and disrupts the way data management has been conducted. This scenario focuses on the strengths of each technology and utilizes the strengths of Hadoop and the data warehouse so that organizations can further take advantage of their data.

Figure 5.4 illustrates step-by-step how it could work for your organization:

1. All of your data—structured and semi-structured—are processed and integrated in Hadoop. Hadoop is now the central

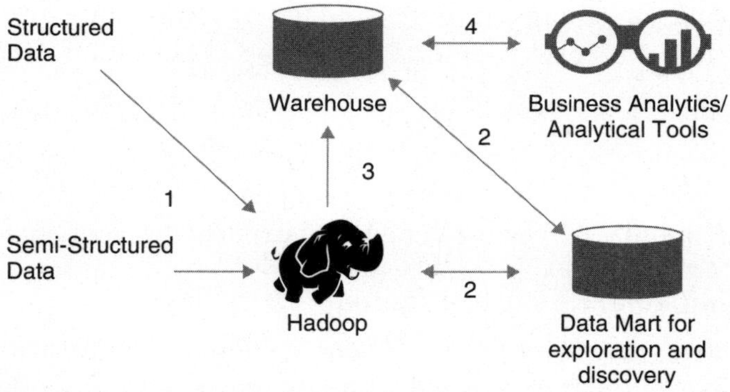

Figure 5.4 Hadoop for data exploration and discovery

hub to load cleansed and integrated data into the enterprise data warehouse. Because the strength of Hadoop is to store all data in their raw and native state, it can be formatted upon request. While the traditional data warehouse requires some sort of data integration upfront, the Hadoop architecture does not. It promotes late-binding concept, a process of formatting the data at the time of the query is requested. In addition, business users do not have to wait for the data warehousing team perform the ETL process and model the data. This process can take days or weeks.

2. In this step, it can get a bit complex, depending on your business needs. The intent for this step is to leverage a data mart for quick analytical analysis for a line of business or department that needs near-real-time analysis. For example, you can load some of your data (whether structured or semi-structured) into your data mart from Hadoop and the traditional data from the warehouse. Once loaded, use your analytical tools to develop the data models or compute intensive advanced analytics processes. Once it is completed, the results can be loaded back into the data warehouse or Hadoop. The purpose for this data mart is exploratory analysis, data-intensive processing of analytic models, and high volume, low-latency, near-real-time workloads.
3. Deciding what to load into your data warehouse is essential for this step in this scenario. Not all data should be loaded into the data warehouse. The purpose of this data warehouse is an efficient and scalable platform for managing core business data and information. The enterprise data warehouse supports many use cases and addresses 95 percent of business intelligence, dashboards, and scorecards to monitor performance management.
4. Once the data are loaded from Hadoop and/or the data mart, you now have a holistic view of the data in your enterprise data warehouse. By incorporating the structured and semi-structured data and analyses, the data warehouse is ideal for storing important data, and for delivery of information to the enterprise.

In Figure 5.4, benefits include the following:

Raw data in low-cost storage

The strength and advantage of Hadoop is to store raw data in its native state. Once the data are captured, they do not need to be formatted immediately. The data can be formatted at the time of the request from the user.

Ability to explore and discover the data

The ability to explore and discover the data can be very advantageous. It allows you to know what you have or don't have so that you can better assess the data situation. You can also discover the relationship of the data and know the correlation of the data (big and small) with analytical tools. In addition, business analysts can determine the state of the data and ensure its validity.

Added flexibility

Not everything is dependent on the data warehouse. By absorbing the costs of data integration up front, the costs of extracting insights decrease downstream. Now that the processing is distributed among the Hadoop and data mart platform, the data warehouse is not overly burdened with queries. The Hadoop platform enhances the data lake concept and the data warehouse enables the enterprise focus.

Keep in mind that these three scenarios are just a subset of all the combinations possible when integrating analytics and data management with Hadoop, enterprise data warehouse, and data mart. In each of the setups, it is enabling companies to become more data and analytic focused:

1. Harness and explore all of your data for definitive business value.
2. Enhance agility and accelerate the time to value for data-driven decisions.
3. Reduce the cost and complexity by eliminating the silos of application-centric approach.

Now that the architecture is explained and laid out, let's examine how in-database, in-memory, and Hadoop can coexist and be complementary.

HOW IN-DATABASE, IN-MEMORY, AND HADOOP ARE COMPLEMENTARY IN A COLLABORATIVE DATA ARCHITECTURE

Vendors offer in-database, in-memory, and Hadoop technologies. The sophistication and level of integration varies, depending on the vendors. For example, SAS and Teradata offer the end-to-end suite of technologies to enable in-database, in-memory, and Hadoop technologies for analytics and data management needs.

Let's start with in-database processing. In-database processing is offered at all stages of the analytical data life cycle. More technologies have been developed in this area because it is the most mature and offers the most bang for the buck. In reference to the collaborative data architecture, in-database processing can be enabled in all of the three platforms: staging, warehouse, and data mart.

As the name suggests, in-database technology is most used with a data warehouse environment. In Figure 5.5, vendors offer in-database software to help streamline the analytical process.

If your organization relies heavily on the data warehouse as the data universe, then applying the in-database processing where the data are makes logical and economic sense.

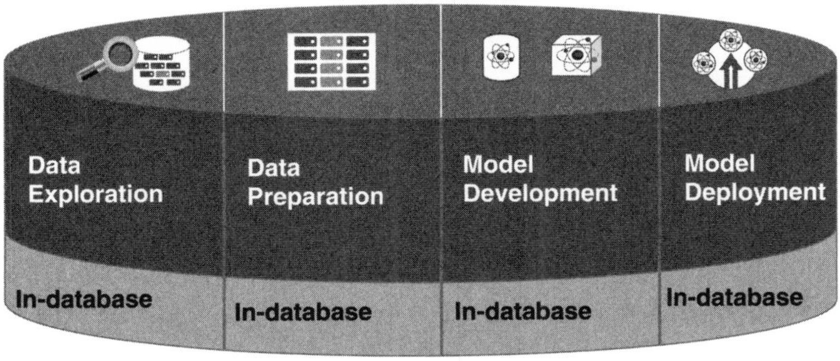

Figure 5.5 In-database processing

Some of the analytical vendors have partnered with the database vendors to integrate the analytical capabilities inside the database. These analytical vendors have tailored their software to run directly on the database system so you can process the data faster. For example, you can explore the data, prepare the data, develop the data model, and deploy the data model directly at the database level. Rather than having to extract a massive data set from your enterprise data warehouse and move it to an analytical server for analysis, now you can run and optimize these capabilities directly within the database. Your data are secured and the results are less error prone because you do not have to pull, copy, and analyze outside the database. Because your data warehouse has the most current data available, you can trust the results of your analysis.

You may recall that Figure 5.5 is the analytical data life cycle from Chapter 1. In-database processing can be applied to all stages of the life cycle. The processes include the following:

- *Data preparation*: There are in-database functions to prepare the data for analytics such as format, frequency, summary, and rank.
- *Data exploration*: You can apply in-database data quality at this stage to ensure that your data are accurate. For example, your abbreviations might need to be standardized or you might have to ensure gender analysis is correct.
- *Model development*: Once the data are in the right format and integrated, you can start to build a data model. Model development can be very complex and often include many variables and data.
- *Model deployment*: The data model can then be scored inside the database as well. By deploying the model logic directly within the database engine, it reduces rework time, leverage the power of the database for speed and performance, and deliver the information faster.

If your company has or is considering Hadoop as part of the mix, you can prepare the data in Hadoop. In this case, your data warehouse workload can be offloaded and shares the processing power with Hadoop.

In Figure 5.6, Hadoop can capture all of your data, and the data can be explored directly. There are a number of vendors in the market that

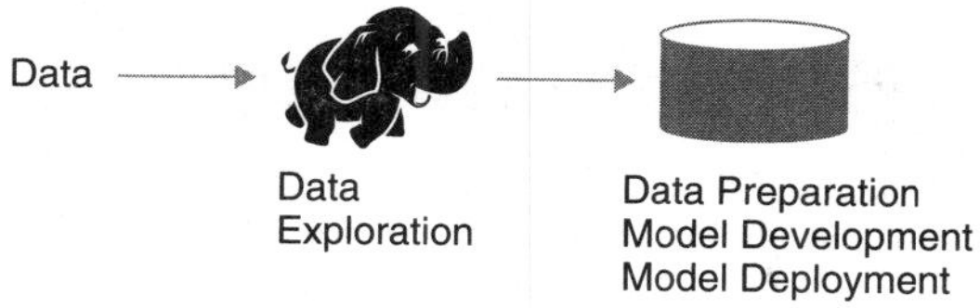

Figure 5.6 Hadoop for data exploration

offer tools to explore data, both structured and semi-structured. Once you decide what data you want to load into the data warehouse, you can then prepare the data and develop and deploy your data model—all inside the database.

To further spread the workload away from the warehouse, you can add in-memory processing on a dedicated appliance.

In Figure 5.7, Hadoop is not part of the architecture. Although Hadoop's popularity is attractive, many customers are concerned about including it in the production environment. In this scenario, you can:

1. Apply in-memory analytics to visualize and explore your data.
2. Apply in-database processing to prepare the data.
3. Build your model using in-memory analytics.
4. Deploy or score your model in-database.

In-memory analytics is very powerful, as described in Chapter 3. If your organization has large data volumes to be considered in a complex data model, in-memory analytics can quickly display all of your data sources within a user interface. As illustrated in Figure 5.7, data are lifted into memory for visualization and analysis. The same is true as you develop complex data models. The appliance that is connected to the data warehouse is dedicated to processing it in-memory to

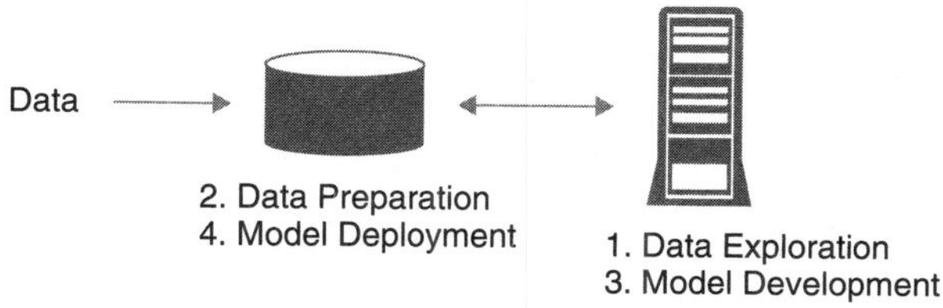

Figure 5.7 No Hadoop

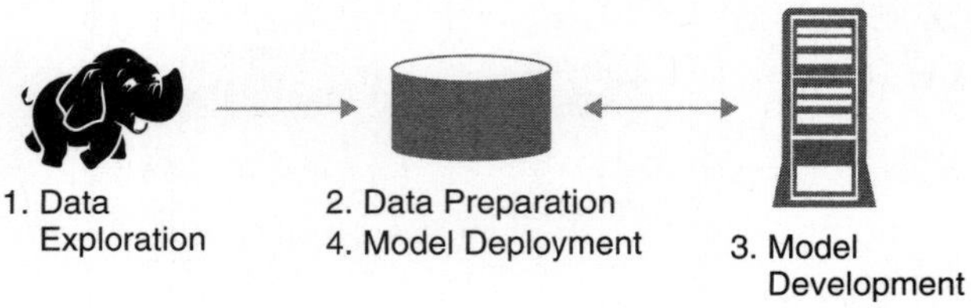

Figure 5.8 Integrating Hadoop, in-database, and in-memory

achieve super-fast performance. The combination of in-database and in-memory can provide end-to-end data management and analytics within an integrated environment (such as the collaborative data architecture).

Not all functions are available using in-database, in-memory, or Hadoop, exclusively, so you may need to combine these technologies along with your current infrastructure to make them work and complement each other for your data management and analytic needs.

The scenario in Figure 5.8 includes all of the technologies to help you:

1. Explore data in Hadoop where all of your data sources are captured.
2. Prepare the data using in-database processing.
3. Develop your complex data models using in-memory analytics.
4. Push the results from the models to score in-database.

Scenarios shown in Figures 5.5 to 5.8 have been implemented by customers in various industries. Let's examine some of these scenarios with use cases and customer stories.

USE CASES AND CUSTOMER SUCCESS STORIES

I want to share with you three use cases and customer success stories that adopt one of the three configurations using in-database, in-memory, and/or Hadoop. As you can see, each customer success story comes from a different industry with a common thread, which is optimizing analytics and data management in an integrated platform.

Large U.S. Retailer: In-Database and In-Memory with No Hadoop

The first success story is a large retailer based in the United States. This customer is a pioneer of the *one-stop shopping* concept. This retailer has hundreds of stores across the United States with thousands of employees committed to excellent customer service, low prices, quality products, and broad selection of brands. Many of its stores are now open 24 hours a day and most stores are open 364 days a year. It offers brick-and-mortar and online services to enhance the customer experience of shopping.

In recent years, the retail industry has evolved and gone through some of the most dramatic changes. This brick-and-mortar business is competing with many channels, especially with other large e-commerce businesses. Today, consumers have so many choices to buy products and services across dozens of retail channels such as drugstores, dollar stores, limited assortment chains, and local mom-and-pop boutique shops.

This one-stop shop sees some top trends that are changing the ways it does business:

Consumers have many choices

According to Deloitte's 2015 American Pantry Study, consumers shop at five different types of stores to fulfill their needs.[3] With so many choices, consumers are buying food and groceries across multiple channels that include supermarkets, supercenters, discount, convenience, membership club, and e-commerce stores. The reason for shopping at multiple stores is mainly due to the variety of value, quality, and brands that consumers are looking to purchase. They can no longer find what they want in one place. With so many choices, there is a need for retail businesses to differentiate themselves to attract consumers.

Price and quality of private labels are appealing

Sales of private labels are growing in popularity mainly due to their attractive pricing compared to more popular and national brands. According to a Packaged Facts survey, sales of private-label groceries are projected to grow 62 percent to $133 billion in 2016. The reason for the dramatic increase can be attributed to the economy and recession since private labels are typically less expensive. In addition, consumers believe that private label products offer the same quality as their counterparts. According to a report from IRI, a market research company providing clients with consumer, shopper, and retail market intelligence and analysis, more than 90 percent of consumers believe private-label solutions offer the same or better value versus their national brand counterparts, and more than 80 percent believe that the quality of these products is the same or better.[4]

Fresh products attract consumers

Surprisingly, fresh produce is a primary driver for consumers in deciding where to shop. According to a Packaged Facts survey, 75 percent of consumers say the produce department is the most important, followed by fresh meat, poultry, and seafood (60 percent); store brand products (36 percent); local farm foods/produce (35 percent); and the in-store bakery (29 percent). As a consumer, I find this statistic to be very surprising and unexpected, as I thought price would be the main attraction for consumers. Growing up in a large family, my parents would look for the best or lowest prices for produce, meats, and other grocery merchandises.

Background

A study conducted by A.T. Kearney found that nearly 40 percent of retailers with loyalty programs fail to use all of the data to fully understand their customers.[5] Even when they do, some retailers who gained that insight failed to ever translate it to action.

With changing times in an evolving market, this customer created an initiative to evaluate data mining tools and advanced analytics to meet the business needs. Specifically, the project focuses on the ability to analyze customers and household purchasing data at the granular level. The project has five goals:

Effectively manage and analyze the growing data volumes

With the increasing number of stores opening and an expanding customer base, the volume of data being collected is growing at a much faster pace. The stores are also adding more merchandise to their shelves to attract buyers with national and private brands. In addition, they want to expand their loyalty customer program with specific offers and incentives for shopping at their stores. Not only has the volume of the data for their data warehouse increased, the types of data collected has grown as well. The size of their enterprise data warehouse has expanded by 25 percent. Thus, a new way of managing the volume growth is needed. In addition, the enterprise data warehouse system is overburdened with queries and analysis that it is taking the retailer longer than expected to execute its analytical processes and reporting needs. With the current infrastructure, the data are not managed effectively to enable a data-driven organization.

Streamline the analytic workflow

The current analytic workflow is too complex. Out of the five goals, the customer is laser focused on this one because it is the most important area for the company. The current analytic approach is very elementary, and the retailer wants to widely adopt analytics across the enterprise to deliver data-driven decisions. This one-stop shop wants to evolve from basic reporting and analysis to advanced analytics that include data model development, deployment, and data visualization by using all of its data that reside in the enterprise data warehouse. The current analytics process is too cumbersome, and they can only analyze a subset of the data because of the analytic application. In addition, the analytic team consists of data scientists and statisticians who are spending too much time manipulating the data and not really doing the core of analytics. For example, it takes several days for the team to extract the data from the data warehouse to the user's personal computer for analysis. During this process, the data scientists and statisticians are having to preparing the data in a form that is compatible for analytics. Preparing the data includes standardizing the data sources, integrating all data sources for consistency, and formatting the data for analytical purposes. The analytical team is spending about 80 percent of its time dealing with these mundane tasks while it should be focusing on the analytics side. Transforming the business into a data-driven company with advanced analytics is the ultimate goal for this retailer.

Improve scalability and performance

The amount of data stored in a database has a great impact on its performance. As mentioned earlier, the enterprise data warehouse is the system that stores all of the data for this customer. It is, however, no surprise that the queries get slower when the data volume grows. All analytics, reporting, and analysis rely on the enterprise data warehouse, and there are many users that touch this system through the day, weeks, and year. Since many of its stores operate 24 hours a day and 364 days in a year (with only Christmas off), the scalability and performance for the data analysis is an issue. Moving the data through the network from the data warehouse to their personal computer is a common practice that creates many headaches for the company. Not only does it create bottlenecks in the network but also analyses of the data can take weeks and days to complete. The personal computer has very limited memory and applications to do what is needed. Concurrent users are querying the data warehouse and constantly fighting for the same resources from the data warehouse. Now that the company wants to embark on advanced analytics, it will require more computations and data-intensive models to accurate analyze the customer base and loyalty program. The current infrastructure is struggling to scale and perform, and the executive team acknowledges that it needs to be improved if the company wants to adopt advanced analytics.

Enhance the need for data consistency

It is common to expect that the data sources come from multiple systems. Once extracted, data should be integrated and loaded in the data warehouse. For this retailer, it is not a standard process. Staff members spend a lot of time extracting data from the warehouse and then manually manipulating it in an effort to meet the reporting and analytics requirements. However, the data source may not be structured to support current analytics and reporting needs. It may not be consistent and formatted in a way that it can be consumed by the business analyst or statistician. More often than not, the condition and granularity of the data are inadequate to support downstream applications if data are not proactively handled properly at the data source. Once the data are extracted and circulated throughout the organization, it is challenging to manage the considerable amount of complexity, and meaningful analyses and reports are eroded. In addition, this customer admits that data quality is not at the forefront and is likely at the back burner (as mentioned in Chapter 2). To enhance data integrity and consistency, data must be cleansed, standardized, and integrated with other data sources. During the data cleansing process, missing values are determined and bad data are corrected. Only after all of these processes are executed should the data be uploaded into the data warehouse to enhance the data consistency. Because this customer has endured the data quality and inconsistency issue, it has impacted the performance of the marketing and sales campaigns and wasted the organization's money, time, and resources.

Invest in human capital

While working with this customer, this is an unexpected initiative that many companies tend to overlook because the bottom line and profitability tend to overshadow everything else. Many organizations say that *their* employees are their most strategic asset, but this company truly means it and stand behinds this initiative. The investment behind human capital extends across its thousands of employees. In its corporate office, IT and analytical team members were leaving for other companies. One of the reasons is that they were not really doing what they were hired to do. The IT team was not really focused on strategic tasks—instead, it was maintaining the ailing infrastructure and outdated systems. More attrition was endured from their analytical team. The staff spent more time doing data preparation and manipulation than analytics. These data scientists and statisticians were not applying their skills to develop and fine-tune the data models. Instead, they were forced to format the data sets, scrub the data, and prepare the data. These tedious and boring tasks were wearing them out, to the point that they wanted more exciting careers elsewhere. This effect trickled down to the business analysts, marketing, and other departments because many of their marketing and sales campaigns were ineffective. Losing good talent and personnel to competitors and other local businesses left a big void at this retailer. It was suffering from having to hire new employees and train them on what needed to be done. The executive sponsor for this analytical project decided that it was time to invest in human capital to keep employees challenged and on board with the company so that they could execute its long-term plans. The analytical team got more involved with the IT architecture so that whatever tools and technology the company adopted, it would meet their needs to support the company's vision. The transformation from just analytics and reporting is now shifted to more predictive analytics for this company.

Overview

The competitive nature of the business and the evolution of the retail industry have directed this customer to expand its reliance and use of analytics for insights that provide a competitive edge.

As the company yearns to adopt advanced analytics with the focus of predictive analytics, it needed a new, modern architecture and innovative technologies to support it. The process and journey led to the adoption of in-database and in-memory processing. It has been several years of evaluating and exploring different technologies and vendors.

In the traditional environment, all of the business analysts, data scientists, and statisticians have to do all of their analytics at their desk. There are a number of challenges with this process:

- Moving or copying the data from the data warehouse to the desktop can be very time consuming.

- Only a subset or small data set can be analyzed due to the capacity of the desktop.
- Everyone has a copy of the data that persists on desktops, which creates data silos.
- The analytical applications that are available on the desktops have limited functionality.
- Data models cannot be developed and scored in a timely manner.

Figure 5.9 shows the process. As illustrated, there are many steps that consume both time and resources. The customer can only transfer a sample of the data set from the data warehouse to the desktop to explore, develop models, and score. By analyzing a sample of the data, it does give you the big, holistic picture of the customer data and profile. In addition, data-driven decisions are executed partially due to the analysis from a small segment. Having a partial view of their customer data is not effective when it comes to executing marketing and sales campaigns of their customer loyalty program. With this current architecture, the team can only develop less than five data models and score them per week. This customer wants to expand its analytical capabilities to develop and score tens of models and eventually increase to hundreds of models.

New Architecture with In-Database and In-Memory

By working closely with the customer and understanding their goals, the direction was to explore and adopt a combination of in-database and in-memory technologies, as shown in Figure 5.10.

The shift for this organization is going from just doing analytics to more descriptive and predictive analytics. This retailer wants to leverage descriptive analytics to answer questions such as:

- What happened?
- How many, how often? And where?
- What exactly is the problem?
- What is happening?

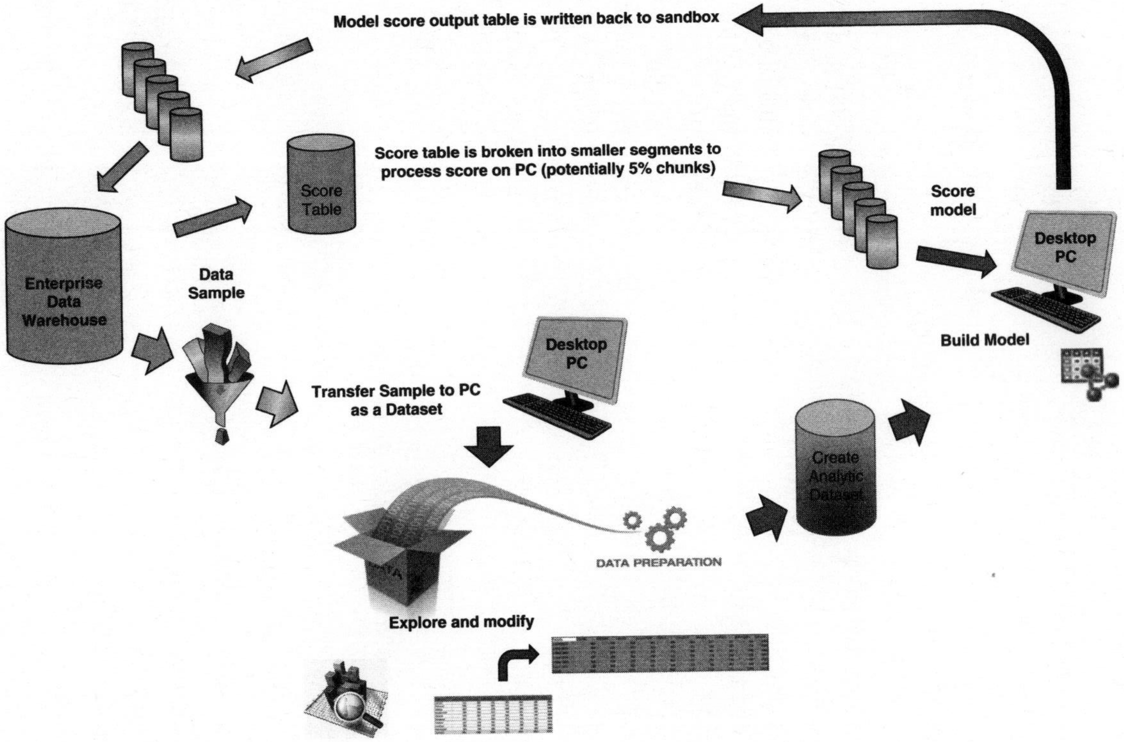

Figure 5.9 Retail traditional process for analytics

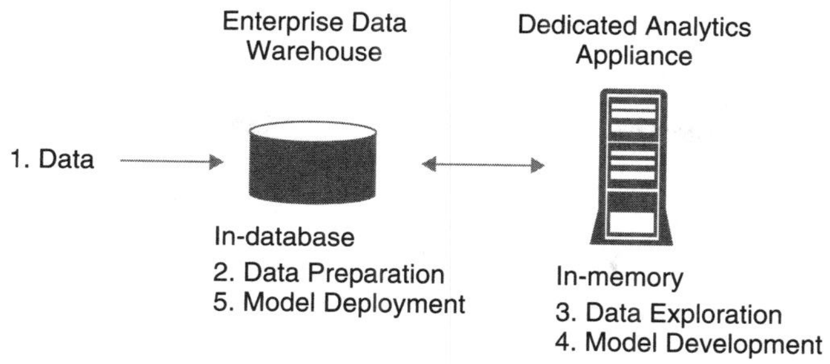

Figure 5.10 Integrating in-database and in-memory

Descriptive analytics assess the past performance and comprehend that performance by mining the historical data to look for the reasons behind past success or failure of a decision. In this case, this one-stop shop wants to use descriptive analytics for business and management reporting—such as sales, marketing, operations, and finance.

Predictive analytics takes a leap beyond descriptive analytics. As the name suggests, it is an attempt to forecast an outcome based on the data analysis. It is using a combination of historical performances from descriptive analytics with rules, algorithm, and various external data sources to determine the probable outcome of an event or the likelihood of a situation going to occur. Like descriptive analytics, organizations apply predictive analytics to answer complex questions such as:

- Why is this happening?
- What if these trends continue?
- What will happen next?
- What's the best that can happen?

Predictive analytics is more sophisticated and requires involvement from statisticians and/or data scientists who can develop algorithms or data models to answer such difficult questions. As previously mentioned, this customer has dabbled in mode development but with limited scope and data to truly call it predictive analytics.

With that objective in mind, the customer wanted an analytical tool that is capable of delivering descriptive and predictive analytics and well integrated with the data warehouse. In Figure 5.10, it got just that.

In this success story, the details will be around a specific focus, which is their loyalty program.

Most retailers, especially grocers, offer loyalty programs. Any loyalty program generates more data and, it hopes, more insights from consumers. The loyalty programs provide a win-win and reward both for the retailer (data) and consumers (in-store discounts). However, it is all about translating this data to understand "individual" purchase behaviors and behaviors outside of the purchase to gain the true meaning of the word *loyalty*.

Let's examine the process in detail to see how this retailer uses advanced analytics to improve its loyalty program by providing personalized offers and rewards to their customers:

- For the loyalty program from this retailer, the data sources going into the enterprise data warehouse include customer relationship management system, market basket, product, and group data. For example, customer data include first name, last name, email address, zip code, and phone number. Product data span a wide range because this is a one-stop shop where customers can buy literally anything they need from food to electronics to sporting goods. As this retailer expands, the data continue to grow in volumes and variety.
- As the data are collected and get loaded in the data warehouse, the data preparation process begins. A combination of in-database functions are applied as well as the traditional methods. Because not all the data processes can be enabled in-database, this retailer needs to maintain some of its traditional processes and complements them with what functions are available in-database. Let's focus on what this customer does in-database to prepare the data for analytics as illustrated in Figure 5.10, step 2.

When preparing the data for analytics, the analysts do the following:

- *Sort the data*: For example, you can sort the data by products or customers.
- *Summarize the data*: For example, summarize the number of customers shopping at a specific store.

- *Rank the product*: For example, rank the top five products sold from the weekly ad.
- *Standardize the data*: For example, standardize the first and last name of the customer by removing variations.
- *Determine the gender*: For example, classify the gender of the customer in categories, such as female, male, and other.
- *Analyze the frequency*: For example, deliver a count of coupons used per trip to the store.
- *Deliver the right format*: For example, ensure that the data set is in the right format for analytics.

The end result of this data preparation process provides the statistician and data scientist an analytical data set (ADS). Refer to Chapter 2 for more details about ADS. The streamlined process with the new architecture from Figure 5.10 shows the technologies adopted and what tasks are performed with the complemented and integrated environment.

- Data exploration (as shown in Figure 5.10, step 3) is executed in-memory using a data visualization tool. This visualization tool helps to further explore the data set for any correlation or relationship between variables. For example, the visualization tool can provide a graphical depiction of average money spent per trip by customer and store. This retailer explores the data in many ways:
  - Examine the most busy stores and peak hours.
  - Show what offers are used by customer.
  - Determine the number of trips made by a customer at a specific store.
  - Uncover what store generates the most revenue.
  - Reveal what products need to be stocked.

  In this scenario, data exploration allows the business analysts to keep what data they want to include in the data model development process.
- Model development (as shown in Figure 5.10, step 4) is the most critical process in this architecture. It is the science that

delivers critical results for this retailer. The data model is used to predict the likelihood that a "household" will make a purchase within a specified sub-category/brand combination. This requires complex algorithm and many data points to support the model. There are two types of data model:

- *Current customer model*: Retain customers in the loyalty program.
- *Potential buyer model*: Expand market basket size by incenting customers to purchase in sub-categories they normally do not purchase within.

The data development is executed on a dedicated analytics appliance. This appliance's primary purpose is to develop complex data models with large volumes of data and many variables. With a dedicated analytics appliance, this retailer is able to develop many more data models compared to the traditional architecture. Currently, it is producing hundreds of models for its loyalty program. All of the power inside this appliance is dedicated to processing the analytics. The advantage of this setup is that it alleviates some of the burden from the enterprise data warehouse because the model development process is on a separate hardware. The team of statisticians and data scientists is able to test their hypothesis and instantly know whether the data models are working or failing. It is a way to easily test a combination of variables and data.

Compared to how the analytical data models were developed, it was taking days and weeks to complete due to the cumbersome process. Now that it is greatly streamlined, model development only takes minutes and hours to complete, depending on the complexity of the model. In addition, this architecture enables a highly governed environment because all of the data used to build the model come from the data warehouse.

- Once the model development is complete, the model can be scored inside the data warehouse (as shown in Figure 5.10, step 5). For this retailer, the results from scoring the model provide:
  - Personalized offers for a specific customer. For instance, customer A is likely to use a coupon for diapers based on past purchases of baby items.

  - Rewards for their loyalty customer for meeting certain conditions. For example, customer B receives a reward if the total purchase is over a certain amount based on five previous trips.
  - Predictions for the propensity that a customer responds to a specific campaign by purchasing a product solicited in a marketing campaign. In this case,
    - The customer has shopped and bought merchandise identified as solicited items within the allocated response period OR
    - The customer has shopped and bought any items within the allocated response period.
- Predict those customers that are likely to respond to a specific campaign regardless of the season such as summer or winter. Thus, the score will select a population to receive the winter campaign since the holiday season is the busiest season for this retailer.

The ability to execute many of the functions in the database and have a dedicated analytic appliance has truly streamlined the end-to-end process for this retailer.

Summary of Benefits and Future

- Achieve faster and more robust analytic insights in less time.
- Accommodate additional workload with existing staff.
- Become more strategic instead of tactical with analytics.
- Execute models within minutes and hours versus days and weeks.
- Develop data models much quicker against large data sets.
- Enable *fail-fast* capability of the data models.

This retailer has made significant human investment. The plan is to hire more data scientists and statisticians to expand the support for enterprise analytics. With the expanded staff, it intends to develop many more data models, beyond hundreds of models to ultimately deliver superior customer experience through its loyalty program.

International IT Company: In-Memory with Hadoop as an Extension to the Data Warehouse

The next success story uses Hadoop as an extension to the data warehouse and uses in-memory analytics for exploring data to detect fraud for the government.

Background

Information systems for governance and public administration have been a high-priority concern in almost all countries. Governance and public administration cannot be productive, effective, and efficient without the support of modern data management and analytic technology. The use of analytics to analyze data and distribute information has been an absolute requirement for public administration and management development. Governments tend to partner with local agencies to provide advisory services and technical assistance in this important area. In practice, however, effective use of information technology and successful development of analytical systems in public sector are not simple. This is substantiated by the numerous government digitization and information systems projects that have failed across the world.

The tremendous speed with which information technology is changing causes misperception, delays, and false expectations for these solutions by many decision makers and government officers. Like the private sector, the public sector has similar issues:

- Confusions about the capabilities and limitations of technologies
- Incorrect development strategies
- Vague development priorities
- Insufficient resource planning
- Inadequate cost estimates
- Misinterpreted user needs
- Selection of wrong products

All of the above often cause information projects to fail. At the heart of the failure is the combination of the technical and management side of the government. Understanding what is the purpose of a government information system and how to develop it successfully is fundamental to government decision makers and managers responsible for their critical areas. The critical issues include: appreciation and understanding of the advanced analytics and data management, awareness of the trends of modern information technologies and their impacts on development strategies, and cognizance of government information infrastructure and information systems development. Similar to the private sector, the public sector is recognizing the value and role of promoting information technology to be used in public administration. In particular, analyzing data to detect fraud is a major focus in the public sector, particular for government agencies to reduce costs and waste of taxpayer's money.

Government programs and operations are vulnerable to a wide variety of criminal activities. Fraud has been a major issue if left unchecked and undetected and can seriously undermine the public's perception and confidence in their government. Taxpayers rightly mandate that public officials wisely use and preserve the money and power entrusted in their government. Social benefit programs such as health care, government loans, and grant programs are all exposed to false claims fraud. Individual acts of fraud and organized ones all add up to huge losses for the government.

Unfortunately, government officials and investigators are largely in reactive mode, chasing the money and the fraudsters after the act has been executed. The need for governments to do a much better job in protecting the integrity of these social programs is essential by proactively stopping the frauds before the money exits the account and before they become widespread and organized. Too often, too many programs are constrained by antiquated or archaic information technology systems. Modernization of these systems should include sophisticated data management and analytics that can enable better, faster detection, and fraud prevention controls to regain the public's faith and trust.

Overview

This customer is an international information and communication technology company for the ministry of economy and finance located in Europe. With more than 30 years of service, it is committed to ensuring the modernization of the public sector by simplifying administrative procedures and increasing integration between public administrations. This IT company promotes the development and innovation through technology to ensure unity and effectiveness of strategic data-driven actions for the government. With thousands of employees, it has designed and built information systems for taxation, self-service analytics, and applications for government departments. This company has cutting-edge technology infrastructure and network to support nearly 100,000 workstations and direct connection with external entities, citizens, businesses, and professionals. Through their efforts, it has created advanced decision-making tools supporting economic and financial policy from a centralized but complex database system. This innovative company cooperates with its customers to ensure high standards of quality and safety and invests heavily in technology, training, and research and development to prepare for the digital age of big data. Its focus in data management and analytics delivers concrete opportunities for growth and rationalization of spending to enhance efficiency of the public information systems.

The customer collaborates with the local authorities for assistance in developing a system to better identify where, when, and how fraud occurs. Working side-by-side, the agency identifies the issues and challenges with the current infrastructure:

Need of insights and timely responses

The government agencies are not getting information that yield to insights in order to respond to critical issues in the tax office, customs office, state property, and minister of finance in a timely manner. Much of their responses to prevent fraud, for example, are weeks if not months after the fraudulent act is complete.

Lack of predictive analytics and self-service capabilities

Business analysts and power users of analytics are limited to what they can analyze. The current tools and technology allow them to analyze only what has happened, and they need the tools and technology to analyze what is likely to happen. Predictive analytics strengthen the ability to detect fraud. In addition, the government agencies lack the self-service capabilities to run reports and share information across different organizations.

Unable to detect anomalies in transactions

The first step to detecting fraud is the ability to report anomalies or strange behavior of the person or business applying for the relevant service or benefit. This process often involves collecting and analyzing the data effectively by using the right tools and technology to alert officials of suspicious claims such as social care, improper health benefits, housing entitlement, and so on.

Dynamically explore large volumes of data

There are many data points to consider when analyzing for fraud that amalgamate to large volumes of data. Considering a sample or partial data sets, which provide a limited perspective of the activities, will not give you a holistic view of the transactions. The ability to explore data dynamically and generate a series of reports will help to find, verify, and investigate people or businesses before fraud can occur.

Centralize analytics and reporting across agencies

Standardizing and centralizing analytics can deliver consistent views of information. It is often an unfortunate case where different analytics and reporting tools are used from silo data and create inconsistent results. Preventing fraud requires a robust process that delivers reliable and dependable information and will alleviate budgetary and resource pressures within the public sector.

Let's examine how this international IT company is helping the local government to improve its process with cutting-edge technology and innovation.

Driving Innovation with In-Memory Analytics, Hadoop, and Enterprise Data Warehouse

The goal of the IT company is to promote and consolidate a culture of transparency and integrity for the public administration. By understanding their needs, it is architecting a system to conduct activities to

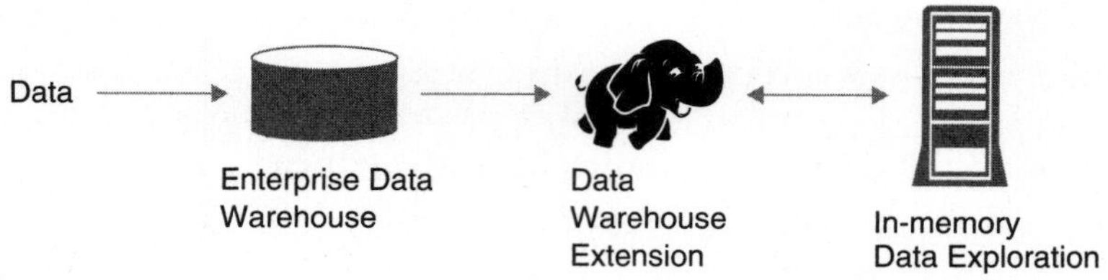

Figure 5.11 Public administration architecture for fraud

improve performance, economics, and governance by identifying the areas that are most at risk and providing support for acquiring a growing awareness around fraud. This company is taking strong measures to prevent and repress criminal acts in the public administration around fraudulent activities. The development of advanced technological solutions will help to achieve its goal (see Figure 5.11).

Data sources for this government agency are structured, more on the traditional side with rows and columns. The data warehouse is the definitive place for all of the data. The enterprise data warehouse has been developed with all kinds of data for decades. Data in the warehouse include census information, household, income, tax collection, and health status, for example. Instead of placing all of the analytical functions and processes on the data warehouse, it has adopted Hadoop to help alleviate some of the workload and performance augmentation. During peak hours of operations, hundreds of users are accessing the data warehouse for various queries and analysis. Hadoop in this scenario is used to extend the value and purpose of the data warehouse for storing data used for fraud-specific analysis. The data from the data warehouse are copied into Hadoop to prepare for in-memory analytics data exploration. This is where predictive analytics come into play. The data are lifted into memory to do the following:

- Provide hundreds of users technology to quickly explore and visualize data for trends and deeper analysis.
- Identify anomalies, irregularities, and fraud in health, gaming, and tax declarations for corporations and individuals.
- Generate reports on fiscal activities, tax collection, health care economics, billing, and use of IT resources by applying predictive and descriptive analytics.

Selecting the right technology and consulting services to integrate data management and analytics with the enterprise data warehouse, Hadoop and in-memory data exploration have allowed the public administration process to be streamlined and effective. The agency is now able to capture anomalies for fraud detection. It is able to do a cost comparison between generic drug and standard product for best and worst behavioral analysis to improve the health care program. It has developed an external web application for all types of users within the government agency to gather more information and define an outlier or anomaly to identify housing tenancy fraud, procurement fraud, payroll fraud, and pension fraud. More applications are being built as they adopt a vision for deeper analytical approach.

Best Practices and Lessons Learned

When the government was considering options in consulting services and technology, a proof of concept was conducted using the resources from the agency. It also leveraged the agency's network and expertise to advise on a standard practice and technology for data management and analytics. The need to centralize and standardize the process and analytics help the hundreds of users to look at the same data and decipher the same results across the government departments. The proof of concept consisted of hardware, software, and services.

Once the government selected the IT company to develop the architecture with bundled software, hardware, and services, it quickly learned that it needed to build the process from the ground up. Many of the users across the government agency were not used to exploring and visualizing the data that they had. They simply took what was there and applied basic analytics to it. Of course, it was often not integrated and/or had missing values in the data to make the analysis effective. In recent years, many customers have leveraged the data exploration process to summarize the characteristics of the data and extract knowledge from the data. They often use newer technologies such as data visualization tools with easy-to-use interfaces at their fingertips to quickly reveal trends and correlations. Visualization tools not only offer users the flexibility of the click-drag-drop user interface, they also have analytical functions for deep analysis of the data.

Building a strong foundation is key. Once you know what data you have to work with, you can use it to build a strong footing for any applications, such as fraud. Basic fraud-detection rules were needed to build an effective system, and the old infrastructure and process did not have it. A comprehensive fraud solution is complex, and many business rules need to be considered to detect the anomalies. Focus on a specific fraud case such as benefit overpayment so that you can show success in one area before expanding.

Let's examine another success story with all three components: in-database, in-memory, and Hadoop centered on an enterprise data warehouse.

National Railroad Company: In-Database, In-Memory, with Hadoop

The next success story is based in the United States and serves more than 10,000 customers by transporting goods and commodities that enhance our daily lives. Being one of the largest freight railroad companies, it employs over 40,000 people and operates across many regions and provinces.

With thousands of miles of track and locomotives, the company has more than 1,500 trains running per day and over 10 million carloads shipped annually. This company has developed one of the most advanced rail networks in the world by optimizing existing rail capacity and making record investments in new infrastructure and equipment directly connected to its operations. The reinvestment into the company sets high standards to improve safety and reliability.

This railroad company is paving its path to the future with analytics. It needs to make sense of all the data that they are collecting. It is applying predictive analytics to enable data-driven decisions to reduce delays and proactively identify issues.

Background

The railroad is a critical element that fuels the economy. No technology, grain for food, or automobile is worth a thing if it cannot move from the manufacturing floor to the consumer's hand. According to the most recent statistic from Commodity Flow Survey, railroads carry more than 40 percent of freight volume in the United States—more than any other mode of transportation—and provide the most fuel- and cost-efficient means for moving freight over land. To support this finding, this customer is able to move a ton of freight almost 500 miles on a single gallon of fuel. This is possible thanks to the technological advancements and innovative sensors in locomotives.

Today, the U.S. freight rail network is widely considered one of the most dynamic transportation systems in the world. The multibillion-dollar industry consists of 140,000 rail miles operated by national, regional, and local railroads. Not only does the railroad system move more freight and goods nationwide, it also offers numerous public benefits including reductions in road congestion, highway fatalities, fuel consumption and greenhouse gasses, logistics costs, and public infrastructure maintenance costs.

The U.S. freight railroads are private organizations that are responsible for their own maintenance and improvement projects. Compared with other major industries, they invest one of the highest percentages of revenues to maintain and add capacity to their system with technological advances. In general, bulk freight such as grain and coal ships in rail cars, while consumer goods such as products found at a neighborhood grocery or department store ship in containers or trailers called *intermodal traffic*. Intermodal traffic refers to the transport of goods on trains before and/or after transfers from other modes of transportation, such as planes, vessels, or trucks.

Almost anything can be shipped by rail. Bulk commodities products such as agriculture and energy products, automobiles and it components, construction materials, chemicals, coal, equipment, food, metals, minerals, and pulp and paper make up over 90 percent of the rail freight business. Intermodal traffic is less than 10 percent, which consists of consumer goods and other miscellaneous products. Compared to other modes of transportation, the rail option offers many benefits. It is efficient at moving heavy freight over long distances. While the trucking industry excels in providing time-sensitive delivery services for high-value goods being transported over medium- and short-haul distances, the rail industry delivers goods and commodities across the country. Raw materials and heavy freight going long distances are likely to continue their journey by rail, or some combination of truck, rail, and water. With the future growth in freight, it is anticipated that freight rail will continue to make investments in technology to increase capacity for long-distance shipments.

Similar to other industries, the rail sector is going through some significant changes and challenges to meet customers' demands. This company wants to offer multiple transportation solutions in a constant effort to be competitive. One area where it sees growth is intermodal transportation, which allows for containers consisting of all types of goods to be placed on rail and redeployed across the country to facilities where they are transferred to other forms of transportations (such as truck, ship, airplanes, etc.) to their final destination. The efficiencies gained from intermodal transportation are even greater with the emergence of double-stacked containers on railcars. With improvements in service and facilities, rail intermodal will become more competitive and absorb the projected increases in freight movement caused by population growth and the growth of the intermodal movement of goods into the future.

To compete in the global marketplace and to enhance quality of life, this customer has made significant investments in technology specifically in analytics.

Use of Advanced and Predictive Analytics

Preparing for growth and the future, this rail company is using advanced analytics to help drive data-driven decisions made by management and the leadership team. With a network of thousands of miles of rail tracks and tens of thousands of locomotive movements to transport millions of containers and products, there is an enormous amount of data to analyze and make sense of data. Advanced analytics can transform data into insights that the business leaders can use to determine how they can increase efficiency and expand the business.

Advanced analytics have become an essential and integral part of the business in the decision-making process. This company is using predictive analytics to uncover the most efficient and safest routes for their trains, adequately staff train crews, proactively order parts and equipment, inspect the trains for preventive maintenance, and so much more. Because the railroad operations can be very complex with so many moving parts, this freight company uses all its data and applies the science to help solve problems. It is also leveraging data to anticipate the changing needs of the business and adhere to government regulations. Another use of advanced analytics is analyzing the shipments of merchandise trains. These trains carry containers of mixed commodities such as lumber, paper, machinery, industrial parts, and various types of chemicals used in manufacturing. By using advanced analytics, the company is able to facilitate efficient movements of these shipments by grouping them based on their final destinations to minimize costs and sorting. In addition, it is able to improve the flow of the products, reduce the amount of time it takes to its final destination, and enhance their customer experience.

Analytics is also used in crew assignment and planning. Like any industry, labor costs are the biggest expense and it continues to grow. For many years, crew planning has been a manual task that takes a lot of time, energy, and resources. Planning and assigning a train crew is a complicated process that involves the consideration of many factors in a short amount of time. The train crew planner has to assign crews located across a large geography in the most efficient and cost-effective manner possible so trains are not delayed or canceled by any means.

This task becomes even more complicated with all the rules and regulations imposed by the government to observe and maintain safe rail operations. An analytical algorithm was developed to assign crew planning in real time in an effort to reduce the overall cost of positioning crews to operate trains within a territory. Once the appropriate resource is assigned, it is also using predictive analytics to accurately predict the arrival times of its trains. This information is shared with customers to track their shipments of products in real time. Customers can now know when the train has left the station, when it is in route, and when it will arrive to the final destination.

Timing is everything. In an industry of transporting goods, their customers are heavily relying on the railroad to get their shipments on time so that they can provide these products to us, the consumers.

Big Data Architecture with In-Memory Analytics and Hadoop

Even though this company is already using advanced and predictive analytics for many of its operations, it is continuously exploring innovative technologies and approaches to analyzing new data sources. Managing big data is nothing new for this company. It has been analyzing large amounts of data for years and relies on advanced and predictive analytics to strengthen data-driven decisions. For example, this company is gathering months of weather data and correlating it to track conditions and/or to track volume to forecast expected conditions. It also leverages video data sources to assess any number of conditions, such as missing or misplaced signs or vegetation growth to alert its field teams where to focus its efforts. To meet regulations or pursue its own continuous improvement objectives, many railroads are combining technology, processes, and shipper training—along with expertise from field-based damage prevention managers—to reduce cargo damage or loss. Rail safety begins with the quality of the underlying rail infrastructure. Maintaining and investing in tracks and equipment is key to preventing accidents. As they move more and more to real-time collection and analysis of critical data, big data technologies allow us to be even more responsive to our business and, in turn, our customers.

In today's data-diverse environment, everything in the rail industry can create an electronic trail of data about its operations and logistics. The analytics team utilizes the mounds of data to generate better inputs for its complex data models and improve its daily operations. New data sources come from sensors that monitor and assist in determining when would be the best time to schedule railcars and locomotives for inspections and maintenance. In addition, it uses data from GPS tools to help track the exact location of their assets. These data sources are detail-rich in nature and can help the company to create effective solutions and positively impact the profitability and its bottom line. Figure 5.12 illustrates the new architecture to support additional data sources.

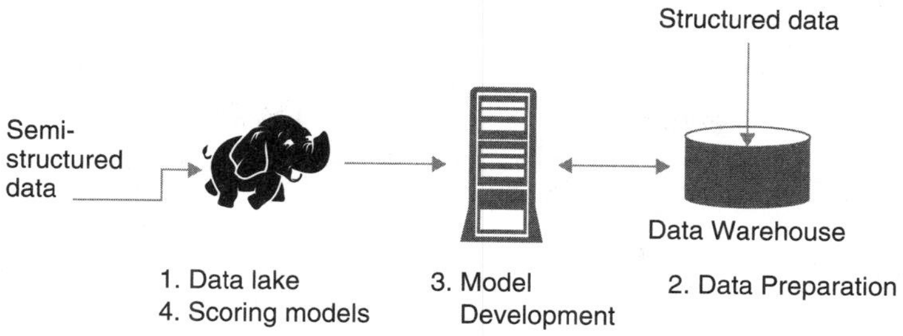

Figure 5.12 Integrating Hadoop, in-database, and in-memory

In this scenario, this customer has invested in Hadoop, in-database, and in-memory technologies to modernized its architecture for the twenty-first century.

1. *The data has two paths*: Depending on the type, the data can go into the enterprise data warehouse if it is structured data. If it is semi-structured data such as detectors and sensors, they go into Hadoop that acts as a data lake to collect a sample of the following sources of data:

   - *Wayside detectors*: These sensors spot defects such as overheated bearings and damaged wheels, dragging hoses, deteriorating bearings, cracked wheels, and excessively high or wide load on passing rail cars.
   - *Acoustic detector systems*: These trackside systems use *acoustic signatures* to gauge the sound and condition of internal bearings and identify those nearing failure. They supplement or replace systems that measure the heat that bearings generate to identify those in the process of deteriorating.
   - *Track geometry cars*: These technology-rich cars utilize sophisticated electronic and optical devices to inspect track alignment, gauge, curvature, and so on. A new vehicle track interaction system is also used to locate difficult-to-find track geometry defects. This information helps railroads determine when track needs maintenance.
   - *Ground-penetrating radar*: This technology assists in isolating below-ground problems—such as excessive water penetration that hampers track stability.

2. If the data go directly into the data warehouse, the in-database process is used to prepare the data for analytics such as joining, merging, and creating the right format. In addition, this customer is taking advantage of the massively parallel processing of the data warehouse to enable bulk load, update, and export large data sets.
3. The data development process combines the data from Hadoop and data warehouse. The data models consist of data from detectors, sensors, shipments, routes, time, crew, and so on. Statisticians look at many variables and situations to develop a comprehensive view of the business. Much of the focus is on detectors and sensors since this provides real-time perspective of the operations.
4. In this situation, scoring the data and models is taking place in Hadoop. Scoring of sensors and detectors data creates alerts for the crews to proactively react to scenarios that can save the company money for outages and issues.

The rail and freight industry uses detectors and sensors to help to improve safety and service, and it is an area of technology with significant investment with high expectation on return of investment. These detectors and sensors generate a lot of data for this company. Detectors are installed under, alongside, above, and attached to the track to find defects in passing equipment, which adds another layer of safety to prevent unplanned incidents. The primary purpose of these detectors is to see, hear, or feel locomotives and railcars as they pass and determine if there are defects. Detector technologies also look for missing, damaged, or defective components from wheels to bearings.

These detectors are generating large data sets daily. There are five types of detection technology, and this company has more than 2,000 detectors collect data 24 hours a day and seven days a week across the system. The data collected from these detectors are analyzed along with other data sources, and the analytics team takes these inputs to develop a data model for predicting patterns and the likelihood of an issue happening to one of its trains. The analysis will help to tweak procedures and business rules criteria for operational improvements. In conjunction with detectors, sensors are the cutting-edge technology that produces many important data points to better manage and identify potential track and equipment defects. By integrating with existing and other types of data, the analysis can provide crucial and critical information about the rail network. By leveraging predictive analytics patterns can be revealed and derailments and outages can be prevented.

Collecting and analyzing detector data is another step toward proactive rather than reactive maintenance. Of course, being proactive can tremendously decrease the unplanned set outs of equipment that can impact velocity and improve safety of responders without increasing risk of derailment. The data from these detectors can augment manual inspections. The inspectors now have additional data points on what to look for and where to look. Ultimately, these detectors focus on derailment prevention and improved safety for the employees and our communities.

The data from the detectors and sensor are helping this company to manage its network to be more on the proactive stance instead of on the reactive position. In addition, it collects a vast array of fixed and mobile sensors to get a real-time view of its assets' condition and usage. Condition-based maintenance and engineering inspection systems will drive reliability in track and equipment, further optimizing maintenance practices. With advanced analytics by using in-memory technology, they will have the ability to model and predict the network impact of day-to-day decisions such as holding or rerouting a train.

The setup in Figure 5.12 serves many purposes for this organization and its customers. For the organization, it will be able to get the information from wherever with any device that includes dashboard and mobile devices. Manual inputs have been replaced with automation. Carrying paper documents and using outdated information is a thing of the past. Documents are automated, smart, and accessible to data and information from any time, anywhere, and any place. Instead of entering lots of data, information is distributed to line of business, managers, and executives. Systems will provide insight to what tomorrow will look like by integrating many different sources for more precise and accurate day-to-day decision making. Touch-, speech-, and gesture-driven applications are in use to better manage the operations. The result of all of this effort behind predictive analytics is that our network should hit new records for safety, velocity, and on-time performance. Working with its customers and partners, it continues to work not only hard but also smart to provide a safe, reliable freight delivery service for our customers.

In addition to organizational benefits, the customers of this freight company are also reaping advantages from predictive analytics. For the customers, data from GPS systems can be analyzed to identify real-time shipment status and more accurate estimated time of arrival. The end goal is to capture customers' needs and proactively know any potential concerns and issues as well as opportunities to enhance customer experience.

INVESTMENT AND COSTS

The blend of in-database, in-memory, and Hadoop requires the most extensive investment. As expected, this combination delivers the highest competitive advantage because of its comprehensive ability to analyze all data sources and deliver greater performance at each stage of the analytical data life cycle.

In most cases, the data warehouse is the cornerstone. It has been maintained over the years to house many data sources for analytics. The investment into the data warehouse continues to be a focus since it provides data for a number of downstream applications for these organizations. There are no intentions to abandon the data warehouse because it plays a critical part of the information system. Integrating in-database processing would be an obvious investment to improve performance by applying analytics to the data directly. In-database processing may not be possible for all your needs, but it can definitely augment the data preparation and analytics.

As mentioned earlier, 46 percent of the users of Hadoop complement it with a data warehouse, and it is often an extension to capture various semi-structured data sources. However, the two customer successes in this chapter use Hadoop for data staging and data landing. All of these Hadoop options help to offset the performance of the data warehouse. Although Hadoop is open source but also an ecosystem, there is some investment for software and hardware. In addition, if you are integrating Hadoop to other systems, it will require additional resources that are familiar with Hadoop to develop and maintain the programming. Since it is open source, there is no user interface to Hadoop. However, there are many software vendors in the marketplace that integrate with Hadoop and provide a user interface to Hadoop.

The investment for in-memory analytics revolves around data exploration and model development capabilities. There are some vertical solutions, mainly in the financial and retail industries. Customers tend to leverage in-memory analytics for high-volume model development and data exploration. When investing in in-memory analytics, it should be integrated with the enterprise data warehouse and/or Hadoop systems so that data can simply be lifted into memory for analysis. If it is not integrated, then you will need additional investment in resources to develop the integration protocol. Not only could this integration development be expensive, it could be time consuming to implement, maintain, and train the users.

Finally, you should carefully evaluate vendors that can provide end-to-end capabilities so that you can simply leverage their software, hardware, and consulting services in a bundle package. It will streamline the number of contracts, vendors, and support that you will have to deal with and can speed up the implementation of the systems if you are on a tight deadline. Vendors that offer this type of bundle tend to be leaders in their respective markets—analytics and data management. Integration between analytics and data management provides optimal performance, economics, and governance.

The next chapter will cover the future of analytics and data management. It provides the top five trends that customers are considering for their organizations based on some of the market trends and the ever-changing dynamics of technology.

ENDNOTES

1. The Data Warehouse Institute, "Best Practices Report: Hadoop for the Enterprise," *TDWI Onsite Education* (April 1, 2015), https://tdwi.org/research/2015/03/best-practices-report-hadoop-for-the-enterprise.aspx?tc=page0.
2. Ibid.
3. Deloite, "The 2015 American Pantry Study: The Call to Re-Connect with Consumers" (June 2015), http://www2.deloitte.com/content/dam/Deloitte/us/Documents/consumer-business/us-cb-2015-american-pantry-study.pdf.

4. Hayley Peterson, "4 Ways American Grocery Shopping Is Changing Forever," *Business Insider* (April 15, 2014), http://www.businessinsider.com/trends-that-are-changing-grocery-stores-2014-4.
5. Joel Alden, Hana Ben-Shabat, Bobby Wehmeyer, and Basil Wuson, "Organizing for Insight: How Retailers Can Collect and Gain Advantage from Meaningful Consumer Insights," *Chain Store Age* (April 23, 2012), http://www.chainstoreage.com/article/organizing-insight-how-retailers-can-collect-and-gain-advantage-meaningful-consumer-insights#.

CHAPTER 6

Final Thoughts and Conclusion

Up to now, you have read and learned what some of the latest technologies can do in the area of data management and analytics. In-database processing can be applied throughout the analytical data life cycle to explore, prepare the data and develop, and deploy the analytical data model in a streamlined process. In-memory capabilities can be applied at the data exploration and model development stages to analyze massive amounts of data quickly and efficiently. These technologies are complementary and can be augmented with the traditional process to optimize the data management and analytics processes. Organizations with Hadoop are integrating with their data warehouse and/or data mart and leveraging in-database and in-memory processing to analyze big data in collaborative data architecture. Organizations are adopting and implementing these innovative technologies together to enable data-driven information for effective analytical-driven decisions. Various customers in banking, e-commerce, government, retail, telecommunication, transportation, and others have provided their insights on the IT and business benefits gained by solving complex problems with in-database, in-memory, and/or Hadoop.

So, what's next in the horizon for data management and analytics? What are some key focus areas in the next five years that will take data management and analytics to the next level? What industries are leaping into the next generation of data management and analytics? Many of these questions will be answered in the next few sections. In this chapter, I will discuss the following topics:

- Top five focus areas in data management and analytics
- Future for data management and analytics
- Final thoughts and conclusion

FIVE FOCUS AREAS

The pace of change is constant, and it is even faster for technology advancements. I am very excited for the future of data management and analytics since every business in every industry is in a position to generate, collect, and explore outrageous amounts of data. There are dozens of interesting data statistics about the explosion of data sources from industry analysts, thought leaders, and IT influencers. They all indicate and expect the amount of data to grow exponentially and beyond imaginable. In one of the statistics, I am astonished to learn that at least 2.5 exabytes of data are produced daily (that's 2.5 followed by a staggering 12 zeros!). This massive data production is everything from data collected by the robots and satellites in outer space to your social media photos from your latest family vacation adventure. Some experts have estimated that 90 percent of all the data in the world was produced within the last two years mainly from digital devices. Looking forward, experts now predict that 40 zettabytes of data will be in existence by 2020. And only three years ago, the entire World Wide Web was estimated to contain approximately 500 exabytes. Thus, 40 zettabytes is beyond conceivable, and IT vendors in the software and hardware business are working diligently to capitalize this massive growth in data.

We (you and me), the users of technology, have partly contributed to this explosion of data. According to a DOMO Data Never Sleeps 2.0 study, thousands and millions of structured and semi-structured data are generated every minute (that is 60 seconds), as outlined below:

- Facebook users share nearly 2.5 million pieces of content.
- Twitter users tweet nearly 300,000 times.
- Instagram users post nearly 220,000 new photos.
- YouTube users upload 72 hours of new video content.
- Apple users download nearly 50,000 apps.
- Email users send over 200 million messages.
- Amazon generates over $80,000 in online sales.

There is no doubt that the increase in digital data is due to the popularity of the Internet and mobile devices and the growing population that wants to join the digital world. As the digital world and users of the Internet expands, new technologies are emerging that allow people to further create and share information in ways previously impossible. Surprisingly, the bulk of data between now and 2020 will be not be produced by humans but by machines—systems that intelligently communicate to each other over data networks leading to autonomous data-driven decision making: for example, machine sensors and smart devices talking with other digital devices to transmit data or machine-driven decision so that we (humans) do not have to intervene. With all of the data points—clicks, likes, tweets, photos, blog posts, online transactions—the digital and nondigital data tell a compelling and detailed story about you and me (who we are and what we do). Hidden in the never-ending tidal wave of exabytes of data are new ideas, insights, answers, and innovations that will redefine the business landscape, drive opportunities for profits, and change business models beyond big data. The challenge, of course, is being able to capture, sort, and use that information in real-time and at scale. This is one of the biggest technological challenges of our generation and the most obvious is the ongoing task of making sense of all that data. So far, however, only a tiny fraction of the data being produced has been explored for its value through the use of analytics. IDC estimates that by 2020, as much as 33 percent of all data will contain information that might be valuable if analyzed properly with the right technology and infrastructure. And, 33 percent of 40 zettabytes is a lot of data!

With the expectations of increasing data volumes, variety, and velocity, adopting and implementing integrated data management and analytics is even more critical to support the needs of tomorrow. Customers across industries around the world have shared with me what is important to them and what they will focus on in the next five years. They are planning to explore, adopt, or implement one or more of the data management and analytic technologies. All customers believe that they can do more with their data and leverage analytics for competitive advantage. They strongly believe that investment in one or more of these technologies will help to maintain their leadership in the market place and drive innovation for meeting the changing needs of internal and external business and IT requirements. These five areas are:

1. Cloud computing
2. Security (cyber, data breach)
3. Automating prescriptive analytics
4. Cognitive analytics
5. Anything as a Service (XaaS)

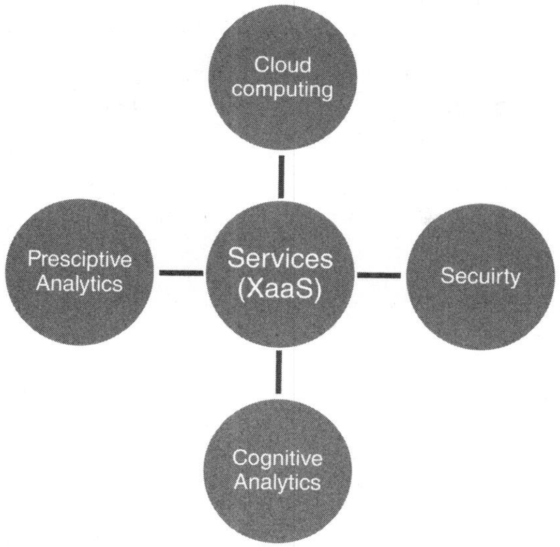

Figure 6.1 Top five focus areas

Most of these five areas are also aligned with the industry trends from Gartner, Forrester, IT influencers, business leaders, and vendors in the data management and analytics landscape. As shown in Figure 6.1, anything as a service is the center of the focus areas that will help organizations achieve their vision for the near future. The other four focus areas (cloud computing, security, prescriptive analytics, and cognitive analytics) are initiatives that customers who I interact with want to embark upon in the next few years. Let's dive into what each focus area is and what it can do to drive innovation for data-driven organizations.

CLOUD COMPUTING

Cloud computing has been a buzzword in the IT industry for a few years now. It is talked about everywhere and by every software and hardware vendor. The global cloud computing market is growing at a fast pace and is expected to reach US$270 billion in 2020. In a recent study, 94 percent of organizations are either already using, or want to make use of, cloud computing as a part of their operations. It is an ideal technology for data management and analytics due to the big data phenomenon (see Figure 6.2).

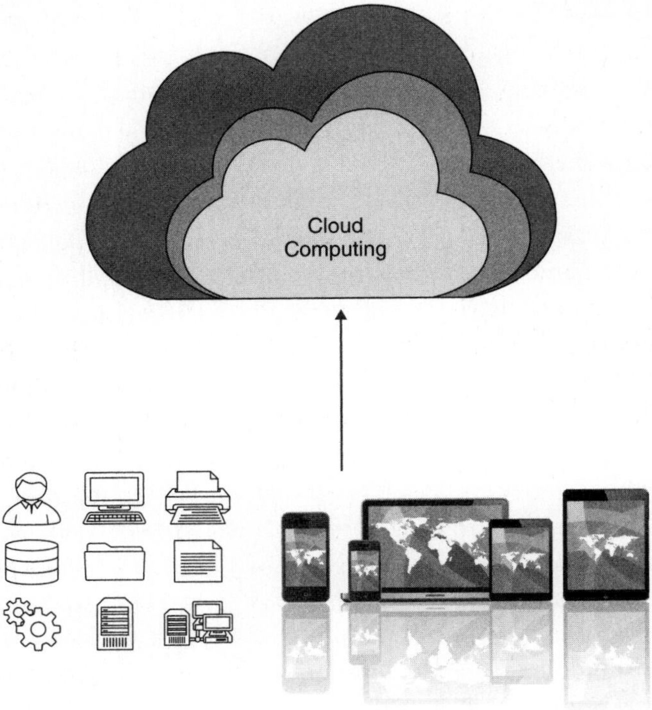

Figure 6.2 Cloud computing

Because cloud computing has been such a trendy topic, there is a lot confusion as to what it is and whether it is anything new that we are yet or not doing. In the simplest terms, cloud computing is a technology that allows you to store and access databases, servers, programs, and a broad set of applications over the Internet instead of your personal computer. Cloud computing providers own and maintain the network-connected hardware and software for applications ranging from business intelligence, analytics, and data management. Cloud computing allows consumers (like you and me) and businesses to use programs and applications without a large upfront investment in hardware and spending a lot on the heavy lifting of managing and maintaining that hardware. Instead, customers can provision exactly the right type and size of computing resources you need to enable analytical capabilities that support your new, innovative idea or operate your

IT department. You can have access to the cloud around the clock year-round, any time, and anywhere, and only pay for what you use.

When discussing cloud computing with customers, I always try to illustrate it with an applicable example. One that is relatable and easy to understand is email, regardless if you have a Gmail (Google), Hotmail (Microsoft), or Yahoo!. All you need is an Internet connection, where you can type in your login ID and password into the application and start crafting and sending emails. The server and email management software is all on the cloud (Internet) and is entirely managed by the cloud service provider: Microsoft, Google, and Yahoo!. The consumers (you and I) get to use the software and enjoy the many benefits.

Traditional on-premise deployments of data warehousing and analytics remain a key strategy for many organizations and the move to cloud computing offers an alternative and modern approach. Cloud computing is providing developers and IT departments with the ability to focus on what matters most and avoid the tedious tasks like procurement, maintenance, and capacity planning. As cloud computing has grown in popularity, several different models and deployment strategies have emerged to help meet specific needs of different users.

The cloud computing services' market growth would be influenced by the global demand for technology-based services, which, in turn, depend on the state of the global economy. Currently, the growth is driven by demand in developed nations in Western markets such as North America and Europe. The developing nations are slow to adapt to the concept, and are expected to drive the growth toward the later part of the decade. The technological backwardness of emerging economies poses restrictions on cloud computing services due to lack of infrastructure availability and technical know-how. Selecting the right type of cloud computing for your needs can help you strike the right balance of control.

Types of Cloud Computing

Businesses have several options in the type of cloud computing and deployment of the cloud. There are three main types that are commonly referred to as Infrastructure as a Service (IaaS), Platform as a Service (PaaS), and Software as a Service (SaaS). Deployment options

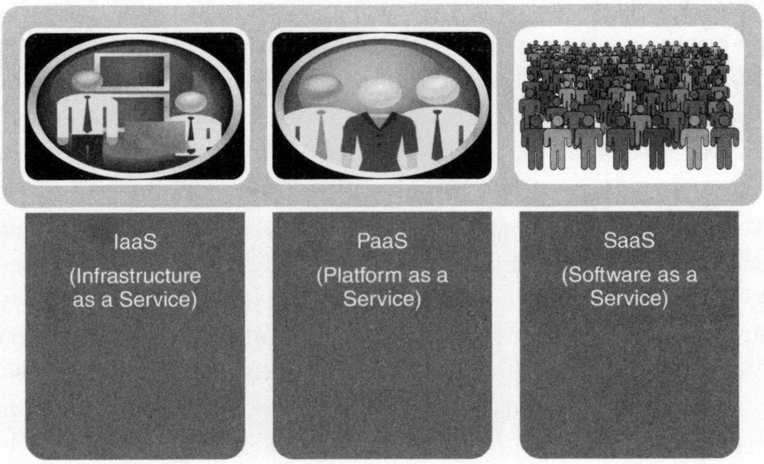

Figure 6.3 Typical cloud computing services

include public or private cloud. Each type of cloud and deployment method provides you with different levels of control, flexibility, and management. It is important to understand the differences among Iaas, PaaS, and SaaS, as well as what deployment strategies can help to provide the right infrastructure for your data management and analytic needs (see Figure 6.3).

IaaS is for network architects, PaaS is for application developers, and SaaS is for end users of all types.

Let's examine the types of cloud computing in detail.

Infrastructure as a Service (IaaS)

IaaS consists of the fundamental building blocks for cloud IT. Sometimes this is referred to as "Hardware as a Service" or HaaS. This means that the service provider owns, houses, runs, and maintains all the equipment used to support operations. This includes storage centers, hardware, data servers, and networking components. IaaS provides businesses with the highest level of flexibility and management control over your IT systems and is most comparable to existing IT resources that many IT departments and teams are familiar with today. Users of IaaS are able to run software, applications, and have control over the operation systems while the IaaS providers manage the underlying infrastructure such are servers, networking, and databases. Instead of having to purchase the hardware outright, users can purchase IaaS based on consumption, similar to electricity, water, or other utility services.

IaaS is ideal for customers who do not have IT resources or expertise in-house to manage network and data management capabilities. For example, IaaS providers can host a data center for you that consists of hardware for data storage (i.e., database or data warehouse), a firewall, and a network for access. Users can access the data server through a secured web interface. In this approach, there is no need to invest in hardware on-premise and maintenance. In addition, there is no need to retain a team dedicated to data management.

Platform as a Service (PaaS)

PaaS provides the underlying infrastructure and eliminates the need for organizations to manage the hardware and operating systems. This means that you will be able to rent the hardware, operating systems, storage, and network capacity over the Internet. PaaS enables you to focus on the deployment and management of your applications. This helps you be more efficient as you do not need to worry about hardware procurement, capacity planning, software maintenance, upgrades, or any of the other heavy lifting tasks involved in running your applications.

These cloud platform services are used for applications and other development, while providing cloud components to software. What programmers and developers gain with PaaS is a structure they can manage and build on to develop or customize their applications. PaaS makes the development, testing, and deployment of applications easy, fast, and cost-effective for the following reasons:

- *The operating system features can be changed and upgraded frequently*: Developers and programmers have more than one operating system and are never limited to one type or another.
- *Developers around the world can collaborate on the same project*: Since developers are running their own operating system, there will never be compatibility or updating issues. This allows the

customer to benefit from the different resources they can obtain from virtually anywhere, anytime, and anyplace.

- *Common infrastructure involves less cost*: They don't need to own individual storage centers, servers, or other hardware. They can consolidate the infrastructure and decrease their expenses.

In addition, application development using PaaS receives the cloud characteristics such as high-availability, high-performance scalability, and more. Enterprises benefit from PaaS because it minimizes the amount of programming or coding necessary and automates business policy for accountability and auditability.

Software as a Service (SaaS)

SaaS provides you with a complete software product as a service. Because of the web delivery model, SaaS eliminates the need to install and run applications on individual computers. With SaaS, it's easy for enterprises to streamline their maintenance and support, because everything can be managed by vendors: applications, runtime, data, middleware, operating system, virtualization, servers, storage, and networking. In this type, service providers host applications that customers can access over a network (usually the Internet). This is one of the most widely used models as more companies are relying on software services for their business. There are two slightly different SaaS models:

1. *The hosted application management*: The provider hosts commercially available software and delivers it over the Internet. For example, email providers like Google or Yahoo! use this model to host their email services and distribute them over the Internet to all web browsers.
2. *Software on demand*: The provider hosts unique software and delivers it to a particular network. For example, a design firm might use this model to host the latest Adobe Suite and make it available to all the designers linked to their network.

This service enables consumers to leverage end-user applications running on a cloud infrastructure. With a SaaS offering, you do not have to think about how the service is maintained or how the underlying infrastructure is managed; you only need to think about how you will use that particular piece software. The applications can be accessed from various client devices through a thin-client interface such as a Web browser (e.g., from Web-based email). The user does not manage or control the underlying cloud infrastructure or individual application capabilities.

Another example is leveraging SaaS for analytics. Users can access the analytic tool to run linear regression, basket analysis, customer relationship management, and industry-related (healthcare, retail, pharmaceutical) applications. Some large enterprises that are not traditionally thought of as software vendors have started building SaaS as an additional source of revenue in order to gain a competitive advantage.

SaaS represents the largest cloud market and is still expanding quickly (followed by IaaS). SaaS uses the web to deliver applications that are managed by a third-party vendor. Most SaaS applications can be run directly from a web browser without any downloads or installations required. However, in the near future all the three segments are projected to experience strong demand and growth.

Deployment of the Cloud

There are various deployment options for you to choose from to support the type of cloud you select. Of all cloud deployment, private and public cloud computing are the most popular. Recent research indicates that 7 percent of businesses adopt the private cloud computing, while an overwhelming 58 percent embrace the hybrid cloud, which is a combination of private and public clouds. While there are three basic types of clouds, there are four deployment options: public, private, hybrid, and community.

Public Cloud

Public clouds are open to the general public with cloud infrastructures that are owned and managed by the cloud service provider. A public cloud deployment is established where several businesses have similar requirements and seek to share infrastructure such as hardware or servers. In addition, it can be economically attractive, allowing users to access software, application, and/or stored data. In addition to the economics, the public cloud can empower employees to be more productive even when away from the office.

Private Cloud

Private clouds are only accessible to the users or partners of a single organization with dedicated resources. Private clouds can be built and managed within an enterprise data center that includes software and hardware. They can be hosted by a third-party provider and managed either on- or off premises (on-premise can be at the company's location). Customers seeking to benefit from cloud computing while maintaining control over their environment are attracted to deploying a private cloud. Private clouds simplify IT operations, on-demand access to applications, and efficient use of existing underutilized hardware.

Hybrid Cloud

Hybrid clouds are a blend of private and public clouds. Customers can choose to create a bridge between public and private clouds to address increased demand for computing resources during a time period such as end of the month or specific peak shopping time such as the holiday season. A hybrid deployment is a way to connect infrastructure and applications between cloud-based resources and existing resources that are not located in the cloud. The most common approach of a hybrid deployment is between the cloud and existing on-premises infrastructure, connecting cloud resources to internal system for additional performance and flexibility.

Community Cloud

Community clouds are comparable to private clouds but targeted to communities that have similar cloud requirements where the ultimate goal is to collaborate and achieve similar business objectives. They are often intended for academia, businesses, and organizations working on joint projects, applications, or research, which requires a central cloud computing facility for developing, managing, and executing cooperative projects. Community cloud shares infrastructure between several organizations from a specific community with common concerns and can be managed internally or by a third party and hosted internally or externally. The costs are distributed across fewer users than a public cloud but more than that of a private to share the saving potential.

Benefits of Cloud Computing

Businesses can reap the many benefits that cloud computing has to offer. These benefits include cost savings, high reliability, simplified manageability, and strategic focus.

Cost Savings

The most significant cloud computing benefit is cost savings. Regardless of the type and size of the business, keeping capital and operational expenses at a minimum is always a challenge to endure and a goal to achieve. Cloud computing can offer substantial capital costs savings with zero in-house server storage, application requirements, and supporting staff. The off-premise infrastructure removes the associated costs in the form of power, utility usage, and administration costs. Instead of having to invest heavily in data centers and servers before you know how you are going to use them, you only pay for what you use and there is no initial invested IT capital. It is a common perception that only large businesses can afford to use the cloud. On the contrary, cloud services are extremely affordable for smaller and medium businesses.

Simplified Manageability

Cloud computing offers enhanced and simplified IT management and maintenance capabilities through central administration of resources, vendor managed infrastructure, and guaranteed service level agreements. The service provider maintains all of the IT infrastructure updates and maintenance and resources to support the architecture. You, as the end user, can access software, application, and services through a simple web-based user interface for data management and analytical needs. No more infrastructure investments or time spent adding new servers or partitioning silos. With the cloud, you basically have access to unlimited storage capability and scalability.

High Reliability

With a managed service platform, cloud computing offers high reliability and high performance infrastructure. Many of the cloud computing providers offer a Service Level Agreement, which guarantees around the clock service with 24/7/365 availability. Businesses can benefit from a massive pool of IT resources as well as quick failover structure. If a server fails or a disaster occurs, hosted applications and services can easily be relocated to any of the available servers within the cloud as backup.

Strategic Focus

If your company is not in the IT shop, cloud computing can alleviate the technological annoyances. There is no IT procurement to deal with, and the high-performance computing resources give you a competitive edge over competitors to focus on being the first to market. Cloud computing allows you to forget about technology and focus on your key business activities and objectives. It can also help you to reduce the time needed to market newer applications and services and become more strategic in focus for your business. Focus on projects that differentiate your business, not the infrastructure. Cloud computing lets you focus on your own customers, rather than on the heavy lifting of racking, stacking, and powering servers.

Disadvantages of Cloud Computing

However, there are some drawbacks and disadvantages to cloud computing, including security and cyber-attacks, possible downtime, limited control, and interoperability of technology.

Security and Cyber-attacks

Customers of the cloud are most concerned about security. Although cloud service providers implement the best security standards and industry certifications, storing data and important files on external service providers always opens up risks of exploitation and exposure. Using cloud technologies means you need to provide your service provider with access to important business data that is sensitive and needs to be protected at all times. Public clouds heighten security challenges on a routine basis. The ease in procuring and accessing cloud services can also give malicious users the ability to scan, identify, and exploit loopholes and vulnerabilities within a system. For example, in a public cloud architecture where multiple users are hosted on the same server, a hacker might try to break into the data of other users hosted and stored on the same server.

Possible Outages and Downtime

As cloud providers take care of a number of customers each day, they can become overwhelmed and may even encounter technical outages. This can lead to your business processes being temporarily interrupted. Since you access the cloud services via the Internet, you will not be able to access any of your applications, server, or data from the cloud if your Internet connectivity is offline.

Limited Control

Since the cloud infrastructure is entirely owned, managed, and monitored by the service provider, the customer has little or minimal control of the systems. The customer can only control and manage the applications, data, and services but not the backend infrastructure itself. You use what is negotiated and provided.

Interoperability and Compatibility

Although cloud service providers claim that the cloud will be flexible to use and integrate, switching cloud services is something that has not yet completely developed. Organizations may find it difficult to migrate their services from one vendor to another in case you receive a better cloud service package. Hosting and integrating current cloud applications on another platform may throw up interoperability and support issues. For example, applications developed on Microsoft Development Framework (.Net) might not work properly on another platform like Linux.

There is no doubt that businesses can reap huge benefits from cloud computing. However, with the many advantages, there are also some disadvantages. I personally recommend that you take the time to examine the advantages and disadvantages of cloud computing, and select the cloud provider that suits your business needs. Cloud computing may not be appropriate for every business but should be considered in the near future for data management and analytics.

SECURITY: CYBER, DATA BREACH

Information security that is data-driven has been in practice for many years and is not a new concept. Regardless of the business and industry that you are in, data breach can happen, and it did. In the entertainment sector, the cyber-attack that happened to Sony breached the internal servers accessing internal financial reports, top executives' embarrassing emails, private employee health data, and even new, yet-to-be-released movies and scripts. This information was leaked and placed on the Internet for public consumption. In the government sector, the U.S. Office of Personnel Management (OPM) was hacked and exposed personal records, including name, address, social security numbers, and background checks on millions of people. Among the details of this data breach were copies of millions of sets of fingerprints. In the financial industry, the cyber-attack seized data from millions of customers of Wall Street giant J.P. Morgan Chase, revealing names, addresses, and phone numbers of millions of household and small-business accounts. Finally, in the healthcare industry, Anthem, Inc. experienced a very sophisticated external cyber-attack, which resulted in the theft of personal information such as medical ID numbers, social security numbers, income information, and contact details from millions of customers and subscribers. As a result, 2.5 billion personal records from cyber-attacks were exposed in the past five years.

Data is a strategic asset as mentioned in the previous chapter and should be protected by all means necessary. Using analytics to detect anomalies for IT security is a common practice. For example, financial services sector companies such as Visa, MasterCard, and American Express have used data and analytics to detect potentially fraudulent transactions based on patterns and pattern recognition across millions of transactions. In the public sector, the government agencies have been using data and analytics to uncover terrorist threats and fraud in social programs and detect insider threats, as well as other intelligence applications. Although big data brings opportunities for businesses, it is also being exposed to malicious use from hackers. With additional data sources, hackers are finding new ways to strike corporate IT systems, abusing the big data opportunities for data breaches and cyber-attacks.

The topic of security is very relevant to recent massive data breaches and cyber-attacks. Security has become a main concern of many executives, particularly the chief information officer (CIO) and chief security officer (CSO), due to recent security incidents. In many of these cases, the cyber-attacks have led to very costly data breaches for Anthem, Inc., JPMorgan Chase, Sony Pictures, OPM (Office of Personnel Management), and Target. These types of cyber-attacks are costing businesses US$400 billion to US$500 billion annually. With such costly measures, IT spending around security is on the rise. The analyst firm Gartner anticipates and predicts that the world will spend over US$100 billion on information security by 2018. Another report from Markets and Markets indicate that the cyber security market will grow to US$170 billion by 2020. As expected, industries such as aerospace, defense, and intelligence continue to be the biggest contributor to cyber security solutions since they have highly classified and sensitive data.

Not only do these data breaches and cyber-attacks affect the businesses, but they also affect you and me as consumers, customers, and subscribers to these businesses. If our personal information is exposed, we are at high risk for fraudulent activities such as identity theft, credit card misuse, and false claims on insurance. Unfortunately, many organizations are simply not prepared and lack the right analytics-based approach, strategy, process, technologies, and skillset to deter and prevent cyber security. Since companies and other organizations can't stop attacks and are often reliant on fundamentally insecure networks and technologies, there is a need to adopt smarter defensive strategies. Compared with traditional security methods and efforts for preventing cyber-attack, big data with new data sources bring additional complexity for analysis. New approaches and new ways of thinking about cyber security are beginning to take hold by better capturing the various data points and leverage advanced analytics. Organizations are aggressively looking at data management and analytics for detecting fraud and other security issues by using advanced algorithms to mine historical information in real time. They are responding far more quickly, using platforms that alert security staff to what is happening or what may likely happen, and quickly helping them take action in terms of predictive analytics. In addition to technology enablement with tools and solutions, all businesses big and small must acknowledge the new cyber security realities and requirements by adopting and modifying their practice to embrace an early detection methodology with rapid response and coordination strategy.

Security Gaps in the Traditional Approach

The historical dump-and-analyze approach has proven ineffective because the needed data history is not typically stored or analyzed in a timely fashion. New approaches are required to leverage and evaluate data in a way that can determine what data is and isn't important to support cyber security–based behavioral analytics. In the current approach, information security is really based on correlating data and events designed for monitoring and detecting known or past attack patterns—"what is happening" or "what has happened." This strategy and tactic have some gaps.

Restricted Analysis on Data Type

Most systems leverage a relational database and therefore require that all of the data be aggregated, integrated, and predefined prior to loading. The requirement to predefine the data and control how the data is sent for analysis can restrict the volume and variety of data that can be collected and analyzed. This also requires significant time managing the data system for end-users as they keep up with updates and change revisions. All of this results in unwanted limitations on the types of security data that analysts see and what they can do to analyze or apply analytics once the data become available.

Delayed Detection of Incidents

As mentioned earlier in Chapter 4 on Hadoop, the database is ideal for certain data types and structures. Combating security and preventing cyber-attacks requires constant streaming of data such as location, physical security information, role, and identity. Leveraging the database to include these additional data requires the process of predefining the data before analysis can take place, which may result in delayed analysis due to integration and customization of the data. These data points and contextual details are essential and can make a difference between offensive versus defensive detection of incidents.

Lack of Ad-Hoc or Real-Time Capabilities

The system is designed to collect, filter, and correlate log events from security devices to detect issues from all the logs and alerts generated. By analyzing the logs with multiple data points simultaneously, the system could identify the most critical alerts to investigate. In order to analyze events across multiple devices, the data must be normalized and stored in a database. However, this design is optimized for detecting alerts but may not be optimized and is less effective for ad-hoc queries to examine attacks that use multiple tactics that span across various touch points and systems.

Rigid Application and Solution

Regardless of the type of company and industry, no two organizations are identical. Every business has different technologies and unique environments, security processes, databases, and analytical applications. Certain out-of-the-box capabilities and reports are adequate, but most organizations need to customize their security solution to fit their environment and business needs. This includes adjusting existing correlation and business rules, developing enterprise dashboards and reports, or generating new ones for added business value. Additionally, nontraditional data sources in the form of semi-structured data (video, blogs, etc.) are often necessary to tackle advanced threats and the ever-changing world of cyber-security.

From a recent survey conducted by ESG (Enterprise Strategy Group), 27 percent of organizations say they are weak when it comes to analyzing intelligence to detect security incidents. Looking at the current status or what has happened model is no longer adequate as multidimensional cyber-attacks are dynamic and can manipulate different tactics and techniques to attain their way into and out of an organization's network and data systems. In addition, the traditional approach and set of security devices are designed to look for particular aspects of attacks such as a network perspective, an attack perspective, a malware perspective, a host perspective, or a web traffic perspective. These different technologies see isolated characteristics of an attack and lack the holistic picture of security. This makes cyber-attacks extremely difficult to distinguish or investigate. Until the entire event data is combined, it's extremely hard to determine what an attacker is trying to accomplish.

In order to combat security issues, building a strong data management foundation for advanced analytics is critical. This entails getting insights into all activities across networks, hosts (e.g., endpoints and servers), applications, and databases. It also includes monitoring, alerting, analyzing for incidents, and then coordinating, containing, remediating, and sharing threat intelligence incorporated back into the monitoring, alerting, and response process. The IT and security teams also need the ability to detect attack activities by leveraging breadcrumbs of evidence found lying across the entire technology stack (e.g., firewalls, IPS, antivirus, and servers). The universal problem is how to be on the offense instead of the defense and to quickly determine the root cause of incidents so that it can be contained before it can be spread throughout the organization. Of course, the obvious intent is to return insight and intelligence from the analysis back into the data system for continuous security improvement.

The French military and political leader Napoleon Bonaparte said, "War is 90 percent information," as he waged war across Europe. In regards to security and the fight against cyber-attacks, this statement is noteworthy and very accurate in today's world. Information that lends to proactive data-driven decisions is critical. Tackling new types of cyber-threats requires a commitment to data gathering and processing and a greater emphasis on analytics to analyze security data. If your organization is looking to embark on or enhance your data security initiative, consider the following shortcomings of your IT system.

Not Collecting and Analyzing All Relevant Data

Today, the limitation for analyzing cyber security is the inability for organizations and cyber software solutions to leverage all of the data assets. Since multidimensional cyber-attacks most likely navigate a variety of systems, networks, protocols, files, and behaviors, companies need to analyze data across all areas. This means collecting from a wide variety of data sources including logs, flows, network packets, videos, identity systems, physical security, and so on, and making them available to all members of the IT and security team. Since multidimensional attacks can occur over an extended period of time, historical analysis is vital and must also be incorporated with the new analysis so that analysts can analyze the root cause and determine the breadth of possible cyber-attack or data breach. With the appropriate analytical cyber solution, context is provided so that patterns and anomalous behaviors can be proactively identified that are indicators of fraud, theft, or other security breach.

Enable a Flexible Data Management System

While original data formats and context should be preserved for integrity and governance, the security team must also have the ability to tag, index, enrich, and query any data element or group of data elements collectively to get a wider perspective for threat detection/response. This allows the analysts to add context to the raw data, making it contextually rich and more informative for proactive actions. In addition, enhancing the data can help alleviate some steps in cyber investigations and become more productive in the process.

Complicated Data Access and Use of Application

Asking questions and the ability to get responses to questions in a timely manner is critical to any operations, especially in security. To state the obvious from a renowned quality control expert, operations specialist, and profound statistician Dr. W. Edwards Deming, "If you do not know how to ask the right questions, you discover nothing." This quote can apply to any industry but is very appropriate for detecting cyber security. Any data—but in particular, security data—will remain a black hole if it cannot be easily accessed, analyzed, and understood by the security teams. To accomplish this, applications must provide a simple, easy-to-use interface to access the data and apply advanced analytics to that data. This will empower analysts at all levels to quickly investigate threats and gain valuable insights. Applications should also allow for uncomplicated ways to develop dashboards, queries, and reports to convey security operations to executives and the leadership teams. Thus, applications with data exploration, data visualization, and advanced analytics provide in-depth understanding of the data and track historical trends across data elements.

Businesses face a stark reality when it comes to protecting their most important asset, their data. The processes and technologies they employed for the last few years are no longer adequate in a world of change and complexity. Sometimes it is better to take a step back and evaluate the landscape of cyber security. This practice will reveal the complex nature of modern multidimensional cyber-attacks and likely convince them to adopt a more offensive, proactive, and comprehensive strategy. Therefore, a vast improvement in security around cyber-attacks requires a robust analytics solution to transform data into intelligence. This means collecting, processing, and analyzing all data and focusing on the people, process, and technology needed to detect and address the security activities. It also includes responding in a coordinated manner to an incident and investigating and determining root cause by scoping, containing, and analyzing the problem. Then bring the results of the investigation back into the application for proactive prevention and mitigation.

This new approach to cyber security prevention can be viewed as an end-to-end relationship between data management and big data analytics technologies along with some consulting services. The technology must be scalable, manageable, and easy to use. Having the right technology and infrastructure is only half of the equation. At the same time, a process is needed for an organization to respond by asking the right questions, knowing how to navigate through the data, and leveraging analytics to stop the hackers in their tracks.

Hackers

Hackers have varying degrees of skills, expertise, and knowledge. According to IDC, there are six categories by which hackers are classified. They are accidental, insider, opportunist, hacktivist, professional criminal, and state-level actors. We will look at these in more detail.

Types of Hackers

A short description of each is defined below:

- *Accidental*: An employee or contractor who works for an organization accidentally and leaves data exposed because of lack of experience
- *Insider*: A more highly skilled employee (compared to an accidental) who is familiar with the internal network and uses known corporate vulnerabilities for self-gain
- *Opportunist*: A third party or external person who, in spite of lacking significant skills, uses basic tactics such as worms, viruses, and other tools (this person likes to brag about their effort)
- *Hactivist*: A true hacker with more experience and sophisticated skills who uses malware to penetrate IT systems; often executed for political stance or with a specific motive
- *Professional criminal*: An organized crime effort(s) from a group including terrorist units that use very high-level and extremely sophisticated abilities to gain financial benefits with damaging information about a business
- *State-level actor*: A person who may be employed by the national government using state-of-the-art techniques to gain strategic or economic information

Harris Interactive, a polling company, recently conducted a survey on causes of data breaches and how these data breaches were discovered. The results are shown in Table 6.1. It concluded that primary cause is from a lost or stolen computing device at 46 percent, followed by employee mistakes or unintentional actions. Ranked third and fourth party are third-party glitch at 43 percent and attack from hackers or criminal at 33 percent. The note on Table 6.1 shows how these breaches were discovered and, surprisingly, over a third came

Table 6.1 Causes of Data Breaches

Cause of Data Breach	Percentage
A stolen or lost computing or mobile device	46%
Employee mistake or accidental actions	42%
Third-party negligence	42%
Criminal attack	33%
Technical system snafu	31%
Malicious act from an insider	14%
Intentional nonmalicious act from employee	8%

Breaches were discovered by:
52% audit/assessment
47% employee detected
36% customer complaint

from a customer or patient complaint. It shows that the company was not even aware of the attack or breach until someone from the outside told them about it.

New Targets for Heightened Risks

The database or the data warehouse remain the primary targets for hackers to penetrate, access, and attack. Once hackers are able to enter the system, it is exposing sensitive and critical information about the company and its customers. In addition to misusing the data, cyber-attacks can really disrupt the day-to-day operations of your company. Hackers often demand a ransom payment to restore access and not to distribute the data publicly. *Ransomware* is not new, but it is on the rise. This is where hackers use a kind of software that can lock people out of systems until they make a payment such as bitcoin. For those who are unfamiliar with bitcoin, it is a new kind of money and is the open source with peer-to-peer networks to operate with no financial institutions to manage transactions.

As already mentioned, it can happen to any company across industries. However, a number of cyber-attack cases occurred in the healthcare industry, particularly hospitals, in the spring of 2016. Hospitals are most vulnerable because they traditionally spend a very small fraction of their budget on cyber security. Aside from having malware and other cyber security software, it is also important to teach a large network of doctors and nurses not to view and click on suspicious links via email. The way hackers get into a system is generally through a phishing attack—persuading any random employee to click on a link or an attachment in an email—or by finding a network loophole. By doing so, it allows its technical systems to be vulnerable to hackers armed with a cutting edge, ever-evolving set of tools. Most of these doctors and nurses are basic users of technology and are not IT savvy enough to detect suspicious emails and what not to click. As hospitals have become dependent on electronic systems to coordinate care, communicate critical health data, and avoid medication errors, patients' well-being may also be at stake when hackers strike. In some ways, healthcare is an easy target since its security systems tend to be less mature than those of other industries, such as banking, retail, and technology. Where a financial-services or technology firm might spend up to a third of its budget on information technology and security, hospitals spend only less than 5 percent. Figure 6.4 shows the cyber-attack incidents by industry.

Hospitals are used to chasing the latest medical innovations, but they are rapidly learning that caring for sick people also means protecting their medical records and technology systems against hackers. It's doctors and nurses who depend on data to perform time-sensitive, life-saving work. Hospitals' electronic systems are often in place to help prevent errors. Without IT systems, pharmacists cannot easily review

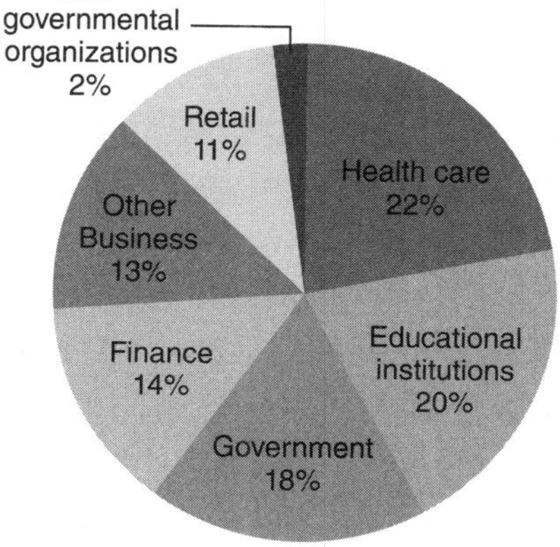

Figure 6.4 Cyber-attacks by industry

patients' information, look up what other medications the patients are on, or figure out what allergies they might have before dispensing medications. And nurses administering drugs cannot scan the medicines and the patients' wristbands for giving the correct treatments. When lab results exist only on a piece of paper in a patient's file, it's possible they could be accidentally removed by a busy doctor or nurse and this critical information could simply disappear.

In several U.S. hospital cases where cyber-attacks occurred, a virus infiltrated their computer systems and forced the healthcare company to shut down its entire network, turn away patients, and postpone surgeries. It resorted to paper records where information was scattered and may not be updated. Hackers were demanding payments in the form of bitcoins to restore the operations of the IT systems.

In addition to the traditional database, hackers are evolving and going after the digital sources such as websites and social media. According to IDC, the premier global market intelligence firm, cyber attackers are aiming at modern technologies such as social media (Facebook, Instagram, Twitter), mobile devices (cellular phone, tablets, PDAs), clouds (private, public, and hybrid), and finally the Internet of Things (IoT), where a variety of digital devices are connected to the Internet (more on IoT in the next section in this chapter).

Vendors offering cyber security are developing advanced solutions, specifically cyber analytics. At the same time, hackers are also evolving and targeting new sources and target areas. They also look for the lowest-hanging fruit of vulnerability (i.e. healthcare and hospitals) to set sights for cyber-attacks. The data landscape for cyber-security is becoming much more complex and CIOs/CSOs are dealing with challenging tasks to protect all data, prevent attacks, and proactively mitigate these threats. Having the right data management and analytic capabilities for cyber-security is only half of the equation. The education and cultural perspective may be harder to solve and maintain. Training staff and employees to not leave sensitive data unattended, not click on links in emails they didn't expect to receive, and report any suspicious phishing activity is a daunting and enduring task. It takes a coordinated effort of people, process, and technology to be successful at addressing security.

AUTOMATING PRESCRIPTIVE ANALYTICS: IOT, EVENTS, AND DATA STREAMS

In the last five years, the term and topic of *analytics* has been trendy across all industries and globally in all regions (Americas, Europe, Middle East, and Asia/Pacific). Companies are making hefty investments in analytics to drive business and operational decisions. Many vendors are spending millions of dollars in research and development to go to market with and deliver the next best thing for their customers. Companies whose domain is not analytics have jumped on the bandwagon to be a part of the lucrative pie. Analytics have become so big that it has surpassed big data searches and should have sub-categories when it comes to this subject. You may be familiar with descriptive and predictive analytics, which have been around for over 10 years. However, the latest trend or buzzword is *prescriptive analytics*, which is the combination of descriptive and predictive. Let's examine the differences in each.

In Chapter 5, we discussed the characteristics of descriptive and predictive. Descriptive analytics assess the past performance and comprehends that performance by mining the historical data to look for the reasons behind past success or failure of a decision. Predictive analytics is an attempt to forecast an outcome based on the data analysis. It is using a combination of historical performances from descriptive analytics with rules, algorithm, and various external data sources to determine the probable outcome of an event or the likelihood of a situation going to occur. Prescriptive analytics is the combination of descriptive and predictive analytics. It takes analytics to the next level, which is beyond predicting future outcomes. Prescriptive analytics prescribe or can forecast what will happen, when it will happen, and why it will happen. It delivers data-driven decision options on how to take advantage of a future opportunity or alleviate a future risk and reveals the implication of each decision option. Unlike descriptive analytics, predictive analytics rely on all data sources, which is a combination of structured (numbers, categories) and semi-structured (videos, images, sounds, texts) data along with well-defined business rules to enable business analysts to identify the actions needed and predict what lies ahead. Prescriptive analytics also utilizes advanced automated data-driven decision—making techniques (e.g., optimization and simulation models) to evaluate the alternatives and deliver these recommended decisions in a timely manner.

Prescriptive analytics require a well-defined process, highly skilled people, and scalable technology. Technology for prescriptive analytics needs to be scalable in order to analyze the multitude sources of data. This technology not only has to analyze all your data sources, both structured and semi-structured, but also needs to adapt to the dynamic of big data of high data volumes, variety, and velocity. The business process consists of business rules which define constraints, preferences, policies, and best practices. Then, the highly skilled people are needed to develop mathematical applications and computational models by applying statistics, operations research, pattern recognition, and machine learning for effective use of prescriptive analytics. Prescriptive analytics is used in scenarios where there are too many options, variables, constraints, and data points for the human mind to efficiently evaluate without assistance from technology. Figure 6.5 is a diagram that illustrates the relationship of descriptive, predictive, and prescriptive analytics.

According to a recent Gartner report, only 3 percent of surveyed companies are currently leveraging prescriptive analytics software, compared to 30 percent that are active users of predictive analytics technology. But with the continued explosion of data volume, variety, and velocity, combined with vast improvements in technology, prescriptive analytics adoption is expected to grow substantially in the next five years. Table 6.2 shows a summary of the differences in descriptive, predictive, and prescriptive analytics.

In the past few years, analytics are becoming more automated as a business requirement and a necessary task. Although prescriptive analytics provides a recommendation to a human to take an action, automating prescriptive analytics take the action on the results of the analysis without having human intervention to act on the decision. For example,

- Prices and packages for vacations change online automatically based on demand or destination.

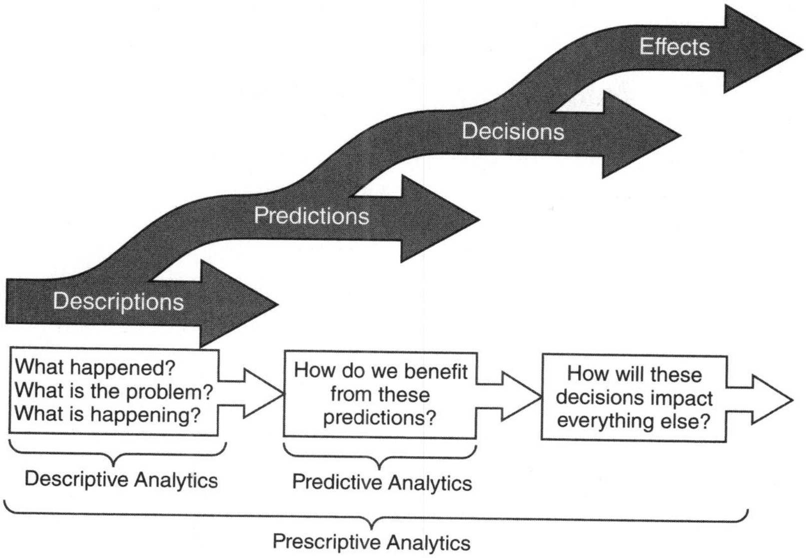

Figure 6.5 Prescriptive analytics

Table 6.2 Different Types of Analytics (Descriptive, Predictive, and Prescriptive)

Type	Description
Descriptive	Used widely by businesses Looks at historical data Transparent use of analytics Easy to understand
Predictive	Expanding use by businesses Complementary to descriptive analytics Test hypotheses for decisions Provide direction for future
Prescriptive	Combine descriptive and predictive analytics Provide results of decision based on scenarios Holistic view from all data sources

- Determine what promotional email to send to a customer automatically based on their preference or profile.
- Deliver a package automatically based on the subscription or membership to a product.
- Send a drone to deliver an order within an hour of purchase.

To its proponents, prescriptive analytics is the next evolution in business intelligence and business analytics, an automated system that combines big data, business rules, mathematical models, and machine learning to deliver sound advice in a timely fashion. The need to automate prescriptive analytics stems from companies that demand real-time responses from data-driven decisions. It is obvious that every company is inundated with data and that data must be analyzed. The reality is that organizations do not have enough people to analyze all the data and make all the decisions in a timely manner. Thus, automating prescriptive analytics makes sense.

The systems into which automated prescriptive analytics are often embedded into the event stream processing portfolio are designed to take action in real time. At the same time, organizations are increasingly enabling prescriptive analytics inside of their data warehouses integrated with their Hadoop environment. This helps with managing their many data sources (structured and semi-structured). An integrated infrastructure that automates prescriptive analytics needs to be closely connected to IT and the CIO organizations. This type of advanced analytics should not be separated or siloed within the organization. Let's take prescriptive analytics to another dimension by automating it in a way that decisions are automatically made without any human intervention.

Value of Prescriptive Analytics

Prescriptive analytics provides the instruction of what to do and—just as importantly—what not to do when analytical models are deployed into production environments. Defined as decisions, they are applied to scenarios where there are too many options, variables, constraints, and data for a person to evaluate without assistance from technology. These prescriptive decisions are presented to the front-line worker—providing the answer they seek and accounting for the detailed aspects of the scenario that they find themselves in. For example, call center personnel often rely on prescriptive analytics to know the appropriate options, amount, and under what conditions, a prospective customer can be extended varying levels of credit.

Prescriptive analytics also provides organizations with the ability to automate actions, based on these codified decisions. Every organization has simple, day-to-day decisions that occur hundreds to thousands of times (or more), and that don't have to require human intervention. For example, the identification and placement of a targeted advertisement based on a web shopper's session activity is popular in the retail industry. In such cases, prescriptive analytics is used to ingest, define, and take the optimal action (e.g., place the most relevant ad) based on scenario conditions (in our example, what has been viewed and clicked on during the session). What is optimal, for the purposes of this paper, is defined as an action that best meets the business rule definitions and associated predicted likelihoods.

Scoring data with a model typically involves IT. Sent in an email, or some of other notification, IT is presented with an equation and the data inputs needed. What is often very lacking is the business rationale, context, and a translation of terminology into IT terms. As such, IT will ask all the necessary questions, often recode the model—run tests and validate output, and then apply any specific business policies and/or regulatory rules—and will put the model into production, that is, operationalize the model so it can generate results.

While in some organizations these steps may not all be done by IT, they still happen. Each step of the data analytical life cycle (as referenced in Chapter 1) adds time to developing the model, implementing the model, and cashing in on the business benefits. In many organizations, the latency associated with model deployment to business action is weeks, if not months. As a result, by the time a model is ready to generate results in a production context, it's often too late—and either the opportunity to impact is gone or conditions have changed to the point where the model is no longer relevant.

Prescriptive analytics have the benefit of automating instructions and best suggested options that are acted on by a person. Prescriptive analytics is also used to directly automate actions, for more mundane tasks, doing so consistently and accurately. In both cases, relevancy to the current scenario is assured in this managed environment and is the product of the vetted, tested, and detailed decision flow. As data volume, variety, and velocity are only set to increase, and as technology continues to develop to process more data, faster—the trend to automating actions taken from analytics will correspondingly rise.

The business need to automate prescriptive analytics stems from companies that demand real-time responses from data-driven decisions. It is obvious that every company will increasingly become inundated with data and that data must be analyzed. The reality is that organizations simply don't have enough people to analyze all the data—even if they could comprehend all the scenario details and volumes, to make all decisions in a timely manner. Prescriptive analytics technologies offer the following:

- Relevant, concise, and accurate decisions
- Easy automation for human instructions and downstream application/system actions
- Explicit use of the business context
- Tested, vetted, and documented decisions
- Adjustability to changing scenarios
- Timely deployed actions
- An unequivocal source of truth, governed in a single environment

Process for Prescriptive Analytics

Being an analytically driven organization means basing decisions and actions on data, rather than gut instinct. As more organizations recognize the competitive advantages of using analytics, the impact can fade as competitors build the same capability. To cross this innovation breakthrough and sustain the competitive advances that come from analytical adoption, organizations continually test and expand data sources, improve algorithms, and evolve the application of analytics to everyday activity to deliver predictive analytics.

Predictive algorithms describe a specific scenario and use historic knowledge to increase awareness of what comes next. But knowing what is most likely to happen and what needs to be done about it are two different things. That's where prescriptive analytics comes in. Prescriptive analytics answers the question of what to do, providing decision option(s) even based on predicted future scenarios.

Events seldom happen in isolation. It is through their interconnections that we develop the detailed understanding of what needs to be done to alter future paths. The richness of this understanding, in turn, also determines the usefulness of the predictive models. Just as the best medicine is prescribed based on thorough examination of patient history, existing symptoms, and alike—so are the best prescriptive actions founded in well-understood scenario context. And just as some medicines can react with one another—with one medicine not being as effective when it is taken with another—so can decisions and corresponding actions taken from analytics impact the outcome of future scenarios.

As you may expect, under different scenarios there are different predictions. When conditions change, the associated prediction for that same data event can also change. When you apply one treatment, you affect another, changing the scenario. Actions that are taken not only create a new basis for historical context but also create new data that may not have been considered by the original model specification. In fact, the point of building predictive models is to understand future conditions in order to change them. Once you modify the conditions and associated event behavior, you change the nature of the data. As a result, models tend to degrade over time, requiring updates to ensure accuracy to the current data, scenario, and new predicted future context.

Well-understood scenarios are fed by data, structured and semi-structured. The more data you have to draw from to examine dependencies and relationships that impact the event being predicted, the better the prediction will likely be. This is where the value of big data comes in—as big data is more data with finer detail and greater context richness. Big data offers details not historically available that explain the conditions under which events happen, or in other words, the context of events, activities, and behaviors. Big data analytics allows us, like never before, to assess context—from a variety of data, and in detail. And when that big data is also fast data (on the order of thousands of events per second), it's a stream of events. When we bridge big data analytics with event streams, as generated in the Internet of Things (IoT)—we have the power to write more timely and relevant business prescriptions that are much harder for competitors to imitate. IoT is a good fit for autonomous prescriptive analytics.

Leveraging the Internet of Things (IoT)

The Internet of Things (IoT) can mean different things for many people and works in conjunction with big data. It is a system of physical objects—devices, vehicles, buildings, machines and others—that are embedded with electronics, software, sensors, and network connectivity so that these objects can communicate through the exchange of data via the Internet. The term was created by a British entrepreneur, Kevin Ashton, back in 1999. IoT is and will continue to generate a lot of data as it represents the connection of the fast growing physical devices and systems. Data transmitted by objects provides entirely new opportunities to measure, collect, and act upon an ever-increasing variety of event activity. According to Gartner, approximately 21 billion connected things will be used globally by 2020. Another staggering statistic is more than 5.5 million new things are connected every day, from sensors on industrial machines to alarm monitoring systems in your homes to GPS location of intelligent vehicles and fitness devices.

The IoT spans a broad range of mature and early-stage technology from RFID tags and remote monitoring to autonomous robots and microscopic sensors dubbed "smart dust". For the record, Gartner predicts that there will be 6.4 billion connected IoT devices in use worldwide in 2016, and 21 billion units by 2020. That means the number of internet-connected things could triple over the next five years.

A respected U.S. president, Theodore Roosevelt, once said, "In any moment of decision, the best thing you can do is the right thing, the next best thing is the wrong thing, and the worst thing you can do is nothing." Decisions with limited information are a thing of the past. The IoT is enabling data-driven decisions with a wealth of information that has often been overlooked. Connected devices, coupled with advances in data collection and analytics, are giving business managers at all levels more relevant and timely information when they need it than they've ever had before. How that affects the decisions they're

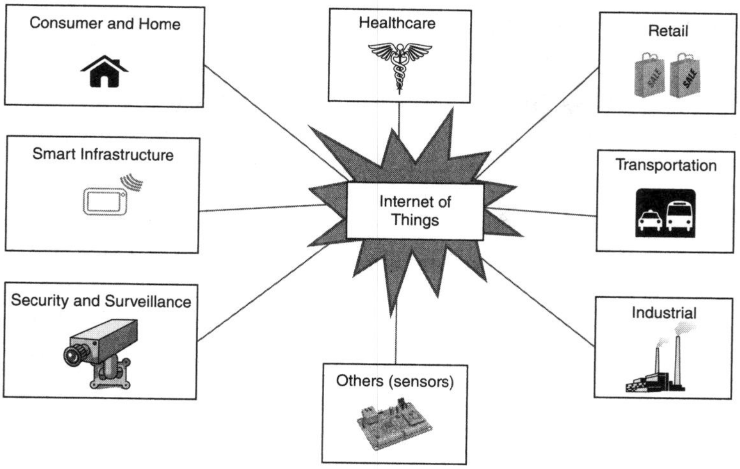

Figure 6.6 Internet of Things connectivity

making is having a deep and lasting impact on operational and business performance.

The Internet is now embedded into houses, vending machines, factory equipment, cars, security systems, and more, as illustrated in Figure 6.6. The connected world can be smarter and has potential to change our personal life and how we conduct our daily business operations. Table 6.3 shows some examples of how industries can benefit from IoT with autonomous prescriptive analytics.

On the downside, as IoT grows, the growing use of detectors and sensors will excite the hackers and cybercriminals. They can leverage these devices to hack into the systems. Many traditional fraud detection techniques do not apply because detection is no longer seeking one rare event or anomaly but requires understanding an accumulation of events in context. One challenge of cybersecurity for IoT involves constant data analysis, and streaming data events is managed and analyzed differently. I expect advanced analytics to shed new light on detection and prevention with event-streaming processing. Another challenge is the plumbing of the data generated by IoT. An even bigger challenge for IoT will be to prove its value. There are limited implementations of IoT in full production at the enterprise level.

Use cases leveraging prescriptive analytics in IoT applications abound: everything from analyzing social media watch by collecting

Table 6.3 Industry Uses of IoT

Industry	Use of IoT
Consumers	U.S. households collectively have over 500 million connected devices including Internet service, mobile devices, tablets, monitoring alarm systems with an average of 5 smart applications per family.
Healthcare	Smart monitoring systems for patients can alert family, doctors, and nurses when a critical situation occurs; insulin injection trackers and prescription drugs adjusted based on real-time analysis of patient's health—all of which can improve patient care and health management.
Manufacturing	This sector leads the way with IoT. There is a 30% projected increase in connected machine-to-machine devices over the next 5 years, driving the need for real-time information to optimize productivity.
Retail	Automated order fulfillment for grocery replenishing, for curb-side pickups, and to prescribe other goods and products for in-store shopping experience; build customer loyalty and satisfaction.
Transportation	Approximately 24 million cars have navigation systems and Internet access to locate nearby attractions for customers on the road.

tweets, blogs, and posts to determine what consumers are recommending as a service/product to security and surveillance of login sessions and data access for data security breaches—and all else in between. Going beyond collection of data for exploration, and even analysis, prescriptive analytics will not only uncover patterns in events as they occur, but they will be used to take automated actions to prevent unnecessary outages and costs. By sending alerts, notifications, updating situational war room dashboards, and even providing instructive action to other objects, the need for real-time actions has never been greater.

COGNITIVE ANALYTICS

In the previous section, we discussed descriptive, predictive, and prescriptive analytics. Beyond prescriptive is cognitive analytics (see Figure 6.7). Cognitive analytics is combining cognitive computing and advanced analytics into a field of imitating human intelligence. Let's take a moment to better understand cognitive computing. Cognitive computing is the ability to access a vast store of historical data (structured and semi-structured), apply machine learning algorithms to discover the connections and correlations across all of those information pieces and human interaction, and then leverage the "knowledge base" as the engine for discovery, decision support, and deep learning. Cognitive analytics is a field of analytics that leverages the power of cognitive computing to mimic human intelligence with a self-learning feedback loop of knowledge. As expected, data is at the heart of cognitive analytics along with natural language processing, probabilistic reasoning, machine learning, and other technologies to efficiently analyze context and uncover near real-time answers hidden within colossal amounts of information.

Cognitive analytics pulls from all data sources for intelligence. This includes the traditional and semi-structured data from the digital world—emails and videos, images and sensor readings, plus the vast array of information available on the Internet, such as social media posts and academic research articles. This intelligence is augmented to make sense of all the data that are beyond the capacity of the human brain to process. The significance of the cognitive system is that it can adapt and get "smarter" over time by learning through their

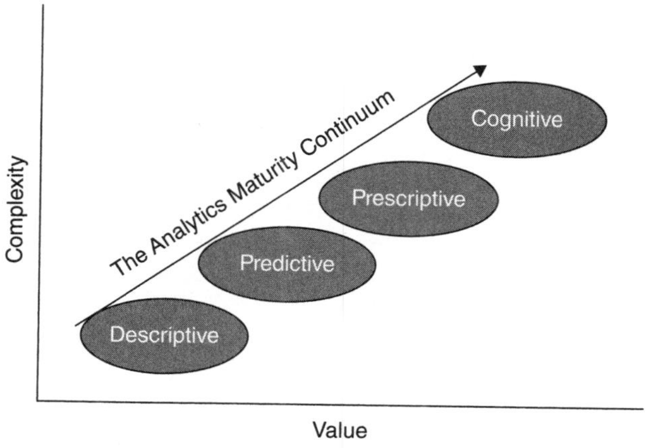

Figure 6.7 Cognitive, prescriptive, predictive, and descriptive analytics

interactions with data and humans via the feedback loop mechanism. In addition, cognitive computing is taking advantage of the technological advancement in processing power and massive parallel and distributed computing capabilities that makes applying the analytics more scalable and feasible to quickly answer complex questions and help us to make even smarter decisions. A cognitive system can provide real-time responses to complex questions posed in natural language by searching through massive amounts of information that have been entered into its knowledge base, making sense of context, and computing the most likely answer. As developers and users "train" the cognitive system, answers do become more reliable and increasingly precise over time. Possible use cases will be illustrated later in this chapter.

Figure 6.7 illustrates the analytic maturity continuum. As expected, the correlation between value and complexity goes hand-in-hand. Descriptive analytics provides the minimum value with the least complexity. Predictive provides additional value as well as increasing complexity. When you complement descriptive and predictive for prescriptive, the complexity and value intensify for matured organizations with data-driven focus. Finally, cognitive involves the highest level of complexity and delivers the most value in the continuum.

With the advancement in computing power and capabilities, cognitive analytics is ideal for data-driven discovery and analytic-driven decision making. This is made possible with machine learning algorithms, which can be applied to all data for mining of historical trends, real-time behaviors, predicted outcomes, and optimal responses. The cognitive algorithms can be deployed to operate in a self-automated way by integrating and leveraging the information from the Internet of Things. Of course, not all applications should be automated and enable a machine to make the decisions, but it is not unreasonable to allow a machine to mine and analyze your massive data collections autonomously for new, unpredicted, unforeseen, and influential discoveries.

Evaluating Cognitive Analytics

The ability to automatically take actions based on data insights is becoming an increasingly important aspect of today's modern business environment to gain the distinct competitive advantage. Here are a few things that IT influencers, analysts, vendors, and system integrators in the industry are saying about cognitive analytics and its future.

Driving Innovation

Cognitive analytics delivers innovation with people, process, and technology. The collection of participants includes computer programmers/developers, data scientists, and analysts who develop algorithms and know how to apply the analytics for the intelligence that can be consumed by the cognitive system. Then, the cognitive system can deliver the analytical-data driven information for innovation.

Transforming Our Businesses, Work, and Life

The presence of mobile devices and the expansion of the IoT are already changing the way we conduct businesses, how we work and live. Business processes can infuse with cognitive analytics to capitalize the big data phenomenon, from internal and external sources. This offers the customers a heightened awareness of workflows, context, and environment, which leads to continuous learning, better forecasting, and increased operational effectiveness. For example, I always have my mobile phone in my possession to remind me of appointments, conduct video and meeting conferences, check on the stock market, access the intranet for company updates, and so on. You may even use your mobile device or tablet for distributing critical alerts to colleagues and customers about a business opportunity or product advice. Cognitive analytics is taking data points from mobile devices and IoT to enrich algorithms and intelligent machines.

The result of cognitive applications includes Alexa from Amazon, Siri from Apple, Watson from IBM, and Cortana from Microsoft. Before long, there will be a marketplace of millions of cognitive agents, driven in part by the explosive adoption of mobile devices, IoT, and the upsurge of machine-to-machine interaction. Examples of such agents would be personal virtual assistants who would be with the people helping in many different facets of life. It will be a foundation to be interwoven into technology (e.g., social media) and touch our daily lives.

Uniting and Ingesting All Data

Cognitive analytics converge and unify all types of data for analysis, human interactions, and digital. Cognitive analytics ingest transaction history, web interactions, geospatial data, web interactions, customer patterns from loyalty programs, and data from wearable technologies (such as Fitbit, smart watches, etc.) at a more granular level. These data points add tone, sentiment, emotional state, environmental conditions, and the person's relationship—these details provide additional value to what have been difficult or impossible to analyze. By continuously learning from data collected, these engagements deliver greater value and become more relatable. Cognitive computing processes constantly run on fresh, new feeds of an ever-growing pool of disparate data sources, including media streams, IoT sensor data, and other nontraditional data sources. One type of data that is integral to cognitive analytics is the open source data. In addition, online community data can provide critical data points for cognitive algorithms to perform with enhanced precision and agility. As data continue to grow with rich context, cognitive analytics becomes smarter and more intelligent in delivering answers to many questions.

Automating Data Analysis

Cognitive analytics is enabling machine learning to understand and adopt new theories and concepts by automating detection and sensing deep patterns and correlations. This automation capability with powerful computing power and advanced analytics is fundamental to machine learning's value in a world where data just keeps getting bigger and grows into higher volumes, more heterogeneous varieties, and faster velocities than ever.

Enhancing Governance

As cognitive analytics drive more business processes and automate more operational decisions, compliance and governance play a key initiative. Organizations are beginning to implement more comprehensive legal, regulatory, and policy frameworks to manage compliance, risks, and consequences for tractability and auditability capabilities. We are seeing an increased demand for more coherent frameworks for cognitive data sharing, decision lineage tracking, and computer algorithm accountability.

In addition, there are safeguards within governance over security, privacy, and intellectual property protection from cognitive systems.

Emerging Skillset for Data Scientists

According to a *Harvard Business Review* report, the job of data scientist has been labeled the sexiest job of the twenty-first century. With the emerging cognitive application development, it has high demand for data scientists with similar types of skills. These professionals are combining statistical modeling, computer programming skills, and domain knowledge in open source technology such as Hadoop, R, and Spark. As cognitive analytics mature, it will require industry subject matter experts to help translate requirements and needs of the business.

Expanding the Need for Services

Every industry's and profession's knowledge is growing at a rate faster than anyone can keep up with. Such as with open source technologies, new protocol, best practices, new regulations and policies, it demands the continuous improvement, adaptation, and augmentation of their capabilities to deliver uses not previously possible. Some businesses that want to explore and enter the cognitive computing and analytics may need to outsource expertise that they may lack in-house in these areas. We discussed the services offered through the cloud, and the same services can be applied here for cognitive analytics. Later in this chapter, we will discuss "Anything-as-a-Service" (XaaS), which can be applicable to outsource data scientists, computer programmers, industry consultants, and project administrators to be on-demand and to assist with the internal resources that may not be available at your company.

Personalizing Our Needs

Everyone likes to have personalization to our likings and needs. For example, when you are sending a marketing email, you often personalize it with a salutation, first name, last name, and a link for more information. Cognitive applications can take the personalization to the next step with more natural interactions such as voice and visualization recognition. In addition, our personal systems will interact with each other, and develop a collective intelligence based on mutual communities and tastes. Analysts and IT influencers anticipate an increase in analyzing geospatial and temporal context of everything we do and deliver reposes based on those contexts.

Cognitive analytics has many possible use cases being explored in theory, which may likely turn into real-use cases.

Possible Use Cases

As I research and learn about cognitive analytics, I must admit I am fascinated with the possibilities and the possible innovative use cases that customers across industries can consider. I covered a healthcare use case under the security section. On the opportunity side, healthcare organizations can leverage cognitive analytics to uncover patterns and make inferences based on aggregated patient records, insurance claims, social media trends, travel patterns, and news feeds. In another example related to healthcare, a doctor or a nurse can leverage cognitive analytics to quickly scan through medical journals, clinician notes, patient history, and other documents to find highly relevant information to improve a diagnosis or treatment plan. Each person can possibly generate one petabyte in a lifetime. Cognitive analytics is designed to help industries such as healthcare to keep pace, and serve as a companion for doctors and nurses with their professional performance. Because these systems master the language of specific professions—for example, the language of medicine, medical procedures, and medical practices, this reduces the time required for a professional or a new medical student graduate to become an expert.

In the oil industry, cognitive analytics can possibly automate operations where there is a lot of streaming data at very fast velocity when monitoring oil fields remotely. This approach can cut operation and maintenance costs, allowing the company to do more strategic tasks. In the digital oil field, a single system captures data from well-head flow monitors, seismic sensors, and satellite telemetry systems, which are part of the Internet of Things. The data are transmitted, streamed, and relayed to a real-time operations center that monitors and analyzes the data to detect anomalies. As the analyses occur, it can automatically adjust these parameters to tame the anomalies, predict downtime, and act on that information to optimize production and minimize downtime. Furthermore, the feedback loop mechanism can train the system to know what to do in the future when a similar incident occurs.

In the manufacturing sector, innovative companies conduct complex analyses to determine how much customers are willing to pay for certain features and to understand which features are most important for success in the market. For example, one manufacturer used customer insights data gathered through sensors and detectors, which are also part of the IoT, to eliminate unnecessary costly features. Cognitive analytics can determine which features had higher value to the customer and which customer is willing to pay a higher premium for them.

Finally, any retail business with a call center can also leverage cognitive analytics. A customer representative can quickly respond to a customer's inquiry about baby gear and accessories by using a cognitive system that pulls information from product descriptions, customer reviews, sales histories, community blogs, and parenting magazines. Like myself, anyone who has a new baby has many questions, concerns, and inquiries about product safety, popularity, and adoption so that you have the best items for your loved ones. Other examples using cognitive analytics include property management where smart buildings are constructed with sensors and detectors via IoT to conserve energy consumption, enhance security for property owners, and perform preventative maintenance on a building or complex.

It is an exciting field. With advancements in technology such as analytics, data management, machine learning, and natural language processing, it is with utmost enthusiasm that I closely monitor and watch the progress of cognitive analytics.

Expectations and Looking Ahead

Cognitive analytics is still in its early stages of maturity and in the mainstream—and is by no means a replacement for traditional information and analytics programs. Traditional analytics and data management systems are based on rules that shepherd data through a series of predetermined processes to arrive at outcomes. While they are powerful and mature, they thrive on structured data, but are incapable of processing qualitative or unpredictable input. This inflexibility limits their usefulness in addressing many aspects of a complex, emergent world, where ambiguity and uncertainty abound. Cognitive systems augment the traditional information and analytics programs.

Rather than ignore unwieldy, diverse data formats, organizations can use cognitive analytics to quickly exploit traditional and semi-structured data—text documents, images, emails, social posts, and more—for useful insights. Cognitive systems are probabilistic, meaning they are designed to adapt and make sense of the complexity and unpredictability of semi-structured data. They can "read" text, "see" images, and "hear" natural speech, which is expected in the modern world. They interpret that information, organize it, and offer explanations of what it means, along with the rationale for their conclusions. They do not offer definitive answers but information that can lead to the right answers. They can be designed to weigh information and ideas from multiple sources, to reason, and then offer hypotheses for consideration. A cognitive system assigns a confidence level to each potential insight or answer. For businesses that need to find real-time answers hidden within massive amounts of diverse data sources, getting a head start on building cognitive analytics capabilities could be a strategic and smart move.

Cognitive analytics will provide additional personalized services to you and me, the consumers of information technology. Based on the data, the details from the results of cognitive analytics reveal our preferences and historical patterns since we are creatures of habits. As humans, we can be inconsistent and unpredictable with our reasoning and decision making. Cognitive analytics can improve the quality and consistency for business and personal decisions by tracing how decisions are made and measuring the resulting outcomes, allowing leading and best practices to be shared across the organization and in our personal lives. Finally, it can enhance knowledge sharing, providing fast access to on-demand answers to highly relevant and important questions. Analytics is about asking—and answering—smarter questions to get higher-quality results at a lower cost. These questions are often about driving more value in your organization, data-driven information that leads to analytical-driven decisions.

ANYTHING AS A SERVICE (XAAS)

We touched on big data and its presence in the marketplace. The growing popularity of the cloud has its collective service offerings (SaaS, IaaS, PaaS). Beyond the cloud, *Anything as a Service,* known as XaaS, in particular, is in high demand to support end-to-end data management and analytics projects. The demand for XaaS plays a critical part in the growing market of big data. According to Accenture, in a study with HfS research, 53 percent of senior vice presidents and above see XaaS as critical or absolutely critical for their organization. In another report from International Data Corporation (IDC), the big data technology and services market represents a multibillion-dollar opportunity in excess of US$48 billion in 2019. With this in perspective, service providers of XaaS are incented to offer software, infrastructure, and platform services in a bundle solution or a single package. The customer can take advantage of XaaS, which can replace traditional services that were provided by one or more IT departments or companies.

With a XaaS solution, the customer receives many services from the same provider for one convenient cost, usually on a subscription basis and often not having to spend any of their capital investment. Not only is this method far easier for the customer to keep track of, but also it provides the customer one-stop shopping. If problems arise with any one service, the customer needs only to contact the company who provides them all instead of having to deal with individual providers.

Companies that take advantage of the XaaS business model will discover that the services are conveniently and largely *plug and play*. This approach is especially beneficial for start-up companies who want to begin immediately without the need to spend time procuring services, managing multiple contracts and moving through the purchasing process. No longer do start-ups have to deal with high and prohibitive costs to begin their businesses. XaaS will allow for far lower start-up costs, as well as the ability to develop and test new business models at a faster rate. With XaaS, businesses can concentrate on the value that comes from helping their customers rather than accessing infrastructure and capital. The managed service nature delivers up-to-date with the very latest technologies and product developments.

In addition, companies can also scale up or down, depending on their needs at a given moment in time which is another important influencer and flexibility adopting XaaS. The XaaS providers bring with it an ongoing relationship between customer and supplier, in which there is constant communication with status updates and real-time exchange of information. This benefit can save a business weeks or months.

Another benefit is cutting out the middle man. The XaaS model is changing everything in that it is both taking over applications and also taking over service delivery channels and thus, cutting out the traditional middle man. With the Internet and mobility becoming the new norm and the standard way of doing things, people can access the services and applications anytime, anywhere, and any place.

XaaS can help to accelerate time to market and innovation. No customer likes deploying something and then discovering that a new or better version of the software or hardware has come along a few months later and they are feeling already behind the technology curve. With the XaaS approach, innovation can occur in near real-time where customer feedback can be gathered and acted on immediately. Organizations (and their customers) are able to stay at the cutting edge with state-of-the-art data management and analytics technologies with minimal effort. This is an area where XaaS distinguishes itself from the traditional IT approach and practitioners who still believe that it's better to build and develop things themselves. There are times that building IT makes sense for the larger enterprises, but it may end up with spending a lot more money to be locked into something that could pretty soon be out of date. Open source and integration environments that encourage application development are thriving. Through this kind of service, the leaders and innovators can be pioneers in their respective markets.

So while the benefits and reduced risks of the XaaS model are clear and tangible, it requires users to have access to a network with Internet connectivity. The network backbone is what powers the XaaS value and proposition forward. These services all rely on a robust network to give the reliability that services need and that the end-users expect and deserve. As companies make the shift to the XaaS paradigm, they must always think about their networks. If reliable, stable, high-speed connectivity is not available, then the user experience declines and the service proposition weakens. Another risk is hiring the right XaaS provider with the right skillsets and expertise. A report published by McKinsey, titled "Big Data: The Next Frontier for Innovation, Competition, and Productivity," cautioned on the challenges companies could face, such as having a shortage of well-trained analysts that could analyze efficiently all the information given by big data. The report cautioned how the United States alone faces a shortage of 140,000 to 190,000 people with deep analytical skills, as well as 1.5 million managers and analysts to analyze big data and make decisions based on their findings.

In today's world of convenience, XaaS can alleviate any guess work with time and resources for data management and analytics projects. Not only do organizations need to put the right talent and technology in place but also structured processes and workflows to optimize the use of big data. Access to data is critical—companies will increasingly need to integrate information from multiple data sources, often from third parties, and have them in a common architecture to enable the value of data and analytics. XaaS can provide the people, process, and technology in many areas. Some of the common XaaS are described as follows.

CaaS

The C in CaaS stands for "Communications" as a Service. You can outsource all your communication needs to a single vendor that includes voice over Internet protocol (VoIP), instant messaging, collaboration, and video conferencing, among others related to communications. In this case, the provider is responsible for all the hardware and software management. Service providers usually charge on an on-demand basis so you only pay for what you need. Like other services, it is a flexible model and can grow as your needs for communication expands.

For example, businesses have designed specific video conferencing products in which users can sign in via the Internet and participate as necessary. Vendors can then bill the business according to its participation. The convenience and utility of CaaS and similar services are rapidly expanding the business world. It is part of a greater trend toward cloud computing services and other remote services used by businesses to reduce overhead or optimize business processes.

DBaaS

The DB in DBaaS stands for "Database" as a Service. It provides users with some form of access to a database, most likely via the Internet, without the need for setting up physical hardware, installing software, or configuring for performance. The service provider manages all of the administrative tasks and maintenance related to the database so that all the users or application owners need to do is use the database. Of course, if the customer opts for more control over the database, this option is available and may vary depending on the provider.

In essence, DBaaS is a managed service offering access to a database to be used with applications and their related data. This is a more structured approach compared to storage-as-a-service, and at its core it's really a software offering. In this model, payment may be charged according to the capacity used as well as the features and use of the database administration tools.

DRaaS

The DR in DRaaS stands for "Disaster Recovery" as a Service. It is a backup service model and provides resources to protect a company's applications and data from disruptions caused by disasters. This service is also offered on-premise as well. It gives an organization a complete system backup that allows for business continuity in the event of system failure. Figure 6.8 shows the types of possible disasters that can occur to interrupt your business operations. Human error accounts for 60 percent of the disaster recovery incidents, followed by unexpected updates and patches at 56 percent and server room issues at 44 percent.

After the DRaaS provider develops and implements a disaster recovery plan that meets your needs, the provider can help you to test and manage the disaster recovery procedures to make sure they

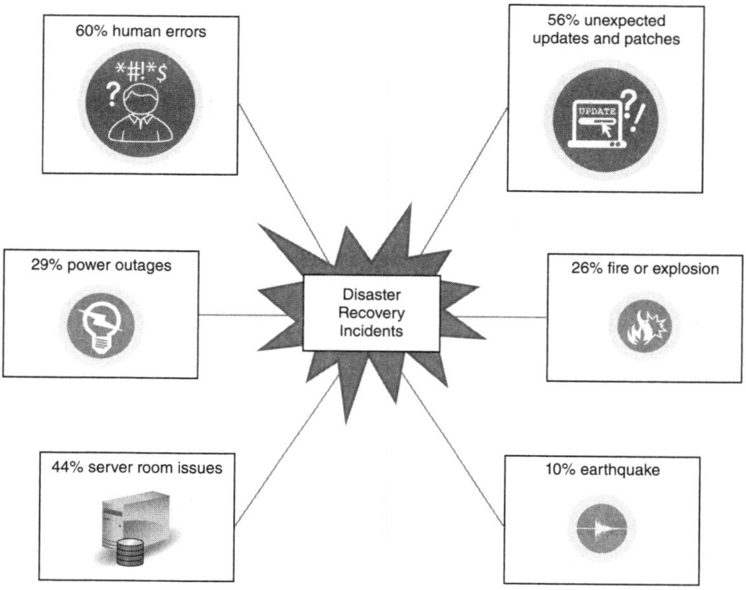

Figure 6.8 Types of disaster incidents

are effective. Should disaster strike, the DRaaS provider also performs recovery services. DRaaS enables the full replication of all cloud data and applications and can also serve as a secondary infrastructure. While the primary undergoes restoration, the secondary infrastructure becomes the new environment and allows an organization's users to continue with their daily business processes.

MaaS

The M in MaaS stands for "Monitoring" as a Service. It is a framework that facilitates the deployment of monitoring functionalities for various other services and applications. The most common application for MaaS is online state monitoring, which continuously tracks certain states of applications, networks, systems, instances, or any element that may be deployable within the cloud. State monitoring has become the most widely used feature. It is the overall monitoring of a component in relation to a set metric or standard. In state monitoring, a certain aspect of a component is constantly evaluated, and results are usually displayed in real time or periodically updated in a report. For example, the overall timeout requests measured in a period of time might be evaluated to see if this deviates from what's considered an acceptable value. Administrators can later take action to rectify faults or even respond in real time. State monitoring is very powerful because notifications now come in almost every form, from emails and text messages to various social media alerts like a tweet or a status update on Facebook.

AaaS

There is one service that I highly recommend customers to consider before embarking on any project that involves in-database, in-memory, Hadoop, and big data analytics. It is the Assessment as a Service that consultants from the service providers can deliver on-premise by evaluating your data management and analytics processes. Consultants who conduct the assessment will meet with your IT and business departments to analyze your data-warehousing infrastructure and assess the analytics practice. This assessment can range from two to five days. The objectives of this assessment are to review:

- Business requirements, time frames, and critical success factors
- Current and planned interoperability between data management and analytics environment, including areas of concern
- Operational data sources to support business priorities
- Analytics and business intelligence priorities, strategy, process, and gaps
- Technologies that are being used for data management and analytics
- Best practices to optimize the analytics and data management ecosystems
- Training gaps and opportunities for improvement in software, hardware, and processes

Before the assessment starts, there is some prework from the customer to provide information to the consultants. The consultants have a list of questions to the IT and business departments on efficiency, productivity, precision, accuracy, empowerment, compliance, timeliness, and cost reduction. Each response provides a metric to analyze the company's current environment and also determine the value within the IT and business departments. It is a well-balanced effort from the customer and the service provider.

During the assessment, the consultants will meet many folks from your organization that can include database administrators, security administrators, enterprise architects, business process modelers, data modelers, data scientists, statisticians, business analysts, and end users. Depending on the number of days for the assessment, each customer will have a tailored agenda. For example, if the customer commits to a three-day assessment, which is the most typical length of time, the sample agenda would be

- Day 1—consultants will meet with IT
- Day 2—consultants will meet with business
- Day 3—consultants will meet with IT and business, share results from analysis, and provide guidance

At the end of the assessment period, the customer will have a technology roadmap document outlining short-, medium-, and long-term actions and strategies for adopting and implementing technologies such as in-database, in-memory, and/or Hadoop to their current architecture. Many customers have conducted the assessment and have found it invaluable to drive innovation, change, and improvement in their data business and IT environments.

Customers have stated that the consultants who conduct the assessment are like marriage counselors between the IT and business departments. They close the gap from an independent voice and provide guidance from an external perspective that many internal staff would have overlooked or not even considered. Their analysis brings fresh, new insights and approaches to IT and business from an agnostic angle. These consultants also bring many best practices from industry specific applications to help integrate and solve complex analytics and data management issues. Customers often ask these consultants to return after the assessment to conduct hands-on training and even conduct another assessment exercise in another department.

Future of XaaS

As the Internet of Things continues to evolve, every business can become a technology company to some extent. Innovative businesses will seek to disrupt their own industries with new and exciting technology products, delivered as a service. XaaS makes it possible for companies outside the information technology industry to deliver these exciting new solutions. With XaaS, businesses are partnering with specialized firms to develop the functional areas and can conduct training that fall outside their primary expertise and focus. Businesses are able to develop new services and products more quickly and bring them to market before their competitors. The "Anything as a Service" approach is really at the center of so much potential business transformation, and it is anticipated that it will become a strategic initiative in its own right. It is creating a whole new paradigm for customers and service providers alike.

Organizations can achieve immediate total cost of ownership by outsourcing these services to a qualified and skillful vendor compared to traditional, on-premises solutions. Overall, businesses are considering and beginning to adopt the XaaS model because it takes the total cost of ownership and transforms it from being a concern into something that is more controllable and attainable. Traditionally, IT initiatives such as data warehousing, business analytics, or business intelligence projects were known for suffering from project delays and possibly overruns. Companies did not know what they would get at the end of a project, which took longer than intended and which was, of course, over budget. These types of incidents would be mitigated with XaaS, and the XaaS approach removes those risks. While there may be a concern about having less control over the whole project or scope of the initiative, businesses have come to realize the benefits outweigh any concerns.

CONCLUSION

In a global economy and complex society where value increasingly comes from data, information, knowledge, and services, it is essential but challenging to make sense for data-driven decisions. And until now, we have not had the means to analyze it effectively throughout the life cycle of data: data exploration, data preparation, model development, and model deployment.

In-database processing delivers the promise of analyzing the data where the data reside in the database and enterprise data warehouse. It is the process of moving the complex analytical calculations into the database engine and utilizing the resources of the database management system. Data preparation and analytics can be applied directly to the data throughout the data analytical life cycle. Benefits include eliminating data duplication and movement, thus streamlining the decision process to gain efficiencies, reducing processing time from hours into minutes, and ultimately getting faster results through scalable, high-performance platform. In-memory analytics is another innovative approach to tackle big data by using an in-memory analytics engine to deliver super-fast responses to complicated analytical problems. In-memory analytics are ideal for data exploration and model development processes. Data are lifted into memory for analysis and flushed when the process is completed. Specific in-memory algorithms and applications are designed to be massively threaded to process a high volume of models on large data sets. Both of these technologies are complementary in nature, and not every function can be enabled in-database or in-memory.

Hadoop is an emerging technology to manage your traditional data sources as well as new types of data in the semi-structured landscape. Hadoop is an open source technology to store and process massive volumes of data quickly in a distributed environment. It is becoming a prominent element in the modern architecture of big data for its benefits, including flexibility with data structures and a lower cost of investment. Many misconceptions around Hadoop have created false expectations of the technology and its implementation. However, Hadoop offers a platform to support new data sources for data management and analytic processing.

Integrating in-database, in-memory, and Hadoop delivers a collaborative and harmonious data architecture for customers with structured and semi-structured data. Customers in various industries implement many variations to take advantage of each technology for their business requirements. From public to private sectors, organizations are leveraging new technologies to better manage the data, innovate with analytics, and create/maintain competitive advantage with data-driven decisions from analytical-driven information. The collaborative architecture integrates data management and analytics into a cohesive environment to improve performance, economics, and governance. It allows you to now crawl, walk, sprint, and run (in a relay) toward success. "The whole is greater than the sum of its parts," as stated by the Greek philosopher Aristotle.

If there is one thing that I highly suggest, it is to review the customer successes and use cases. Not only do they provide information that many of you can relate to, but they also provide some best practices when considering any and all of the technologies (in-database, in-memory, Hadoop). These use cases are the ultimate proof that these technologies are effective, add strategic value to their organizations, and provide data-driven analytical insights for innovation. Whether you are an executive, line of business manager, business analyst, developers/programmers, data scientists, or IT professional, these use cases can enlighten the way you do things and help you explore the many options that may be applicable to your needs. Customer successes and use cases are the most popular requests when it comes to introducing new concepts and technologies at conferences and any speaking engagement. Even when I talk to internal sales folks, they always ask for use cases to share with their prospects and customers how other clients are using these technologies and what tangible and intangible benefits they have achieved.

We are barely scratching the surface when it comes to analyzing data. The future of data management and analytics is pretty exciting and rapidly evolving. Customers are looking forward to refocusing their efforts on some existing initiatives as well as embracing new ones. Some customers may already have a security application in place but with newer sources of threat, it may be wise to upgrade or explore enhanced solution to prevent fraud and cyber-attacks. For others, new focus areas are cloud computing and services. The two are complementary if you want to consider remote data centers, virtual applications, and outsourcing services to fill in the gaps that your organizations may lack. Finally, prescriptive and cognitive analytics are two focus areas that apply automation and machine learning.

I am personally excited for the maturation of prescriptive and cognitive analytics as the Internet of Things evolve. These two technology advancements are complex in nature but they also provide the most value and captivation. Ultimately, businesses will possess the foresight into the increasingly volatile and complex future with prescriptive and cognitive analytics. Such insight and foresight are important to business leaders who want to innovate in their respective industries—on complex financial modeling, on drug development, on new scientific discovery to help cure disease, or on launching a new product or start-up company. Prescriptive and cognitive analytics can reveal hidden and complex patterns in data, uncover opportunities, and prescribe actionable hypotheses that would be nearly impossible to discover using traditional approaches or human intelligence alone. Both require an underlying architecture that is flexible and scalable regardless of the industry that you may be in. This architecture must tie people, process, and technology together to support a diverse set of data management and analytics applications from an ecosystem of data scientists, programmers, and developers. Specifically for cognitive analytics, it must encompass machine learning, reasoning, natural language processing, speech and vision, human-computer interaction, dialog and narrative generation, and more. Many of these capabilities require specialized infrastructure that leverages high-performance computing, specialized hardware platforms, and particular resources with specific technical expertise. People, process, and technology must be developed in concert, with hardware, software, and applications that are constructed expressly to work together in support of your initiative and your organization's livelihood. For me, the journey ends for now, and I look forward to our next adventure—helping you improve performance, economics, and governance in data management and analytics.

Afterword

By Bill Franks

Very few businesses today reject the idea that being data driven and making use of analytics is critical to success. However, many do a poor job of actually becoming data driven and developing the analytics required to do so. One reason for the difficulty is the complexity and scale of the data and analytic processing required to achieve success. It is no small task to successfully capture, analyze, and act upon all of the data available to inform business decisions today.

The methods that were widespread early in my career have proven to be insufficient in today's world. Without taking advantage of the latest tools, technologies, and analytic techniques, it simply won't be possible to realize the goal of being a truly data-driven company. That certainly sounds like an intimidating thing to say, but it needn't be. The fact is that many companies have already successfully adapted to, and implemented, today's best practices. It is also possible for you and your organization to do so as long as you take the time to educate yourself on the options. By reading this book, you've taken a good first step.

In the book, Tho Nguyen provided some very detailed descriptions of the life cycle of data, several key technological and architectural options for analyzing data, and how to tie them all together to achieve success. As Tho made clear, there is not a single "right" answer that covers every type of data, every analytic need, and every business problem. That is simply an unfortunate fact of life when pursuing today's highly complex and massively scaled analytics. However, saying that there is no single "right" answer doesn't mean that it is hard to find an answer that will work for you. By assessing your needs and using what you've learned in this book, you will be able to draft a solid set of plans that will work for your organization.

One thing that the book goes out of its way to do is to provide some examples of organizations that have utilized the various approaches discussed. The examples make the technical points seem much more tangible and help to illustrate the strengths and weaknesses of different approaches. I have always found that the best way to understand how a technical or architectural approach actually works is to review how it was put to use in a real-world setting. By providing the numerous examples, Tho was able to provide important context to the key points he made.

While it has made life more difficult in some ways, the complexity of today's analytical environments has freed us in others. As Tho rightly pointed out, the right solution for any given company will likely contain several different platforms and processing methods working together to get the job done. In-memory processing won't solve all problems today, nor will in-database processing, nor will cheap disk farms. Each of those has a place, depending on the type of analytics required, the volume of the data involved, and the value of the problem being addressed. Rather than making an either/or decision, organizations must stitch together several technologies and approaches and then proceed to harvest the best each has to offer.

In the end, it isn't the technology that matters nor is it the data. What really matters are the results that are successfully derived from them both. This is where the real value of the book is found. As the examples in the book illustrated, incremental gains in analytic power and performance aren't what will be enabled by adopting the approaches in the book. What will be enabled is a quantum leap in performance.

The opportunity is not to take current analytic processes from many weeks to a few weeks or many days to a few days or many hours to a few hours. That would be interesting and possibly even compelling enough to get you to take action. However, such gains are still incremental in nature and in most cases won't fundamentally change the scope of what is possible. What you should be most excited about is the ability to take those many weeks down to just hours, or those many days down to just minutes, or those many hours down to just seconds.

That level of performance improvement enables an entirely different depth, breadth, and frequency of analysis. Just the type of improvement needed to become data driven in fact! The gains discussed in the book are real. I've seen them, and Tho could have added example after example had there been space. He didn't focus on a few extreme examples to artificially inflate his case. He simply picked a representative sample of a much broader set of success stories. With a little research, you'll be able to find many more yourself if you desire.

If you want your organization to maximize its success and become one of the companies that successfully implements a data-driven strategy, you'll need to seriously consider adopting one or more of the approaches in this book. The approaches have been developed, tested, and proven successful by some of the world's largest, most complex, and most successful companies. Tho has been lucky enough to have a front seat to witness what many of them have done. Take advantage of the view he's provided you from his seat as you move forward from the book. Both you and your organization will be well served if you do.

Bill Franks
Chief Analytics Officer, Teradata
Author of *Taming the Big Data Tidal Wave*
and *The Analytics Revolution*

Index